POLITICS: REALISM
AND IMAGINATION

POLITICS: REALISM
AND
IMAGINATION

Michael Novak

HERDER AND HERDER

1971
HERDER AND HERDER NEW YORK
232 Madison Avenue, New York 10016

Chapters 7 and 11 appear here for the first time, as does the introductory essay. The other chapters are based on essays which have appeared elsewhere: Chapters 1, 3, 4, 5, 6, 10, and 16 in *Commonweal;* Chapters 2, 8, 12, 13, 14, and 15 in *Christianity and Crisis;* and Chapter 9, the Introduction in the Schocken Books edition of Helmut Thielicke's *Nihilism.*

Contents

FOR BROTHER DAVID DARST
WHO LIKE MY BROTHER DICK
PRIEST OF THE CONGREGATION OF HOLY CROSS
(B. AUGUST 2, 1935, D. JANUARY 16, 1964)
IS MY BROTHER
AND IN COURAGE AND WITNESS
DIED FOR US.

Preface

On May 17, 1968, Brother David Darst with eight others burned six hundred draft files in Catonsville, Maryland, with a home-made semblance of napalm. He was later sentenced to two years in prison.

In an interview printed in The National Catholic Reporter *(November 12, 1969), David explained how he came to his anti-Vietnam position. The interview jarred me in the pit of my stomach.*

Being exposed to this fierce feeling about the war [on the part of my students at a Kansas City high school, fifteen percent of them poor and black and facing the draft] led me to see that I was kind of out of it, and that I really didn't know the history of it, and that I was not sure of what was involved. So I went on a kind of frantic reading binge: Senator Fulbright's book, some articles, things by Bernard Fall, plus some other material. I remember very particularly going back to two articles by Michael Novak, which I think later appeared in his Theology for Radical Politics. *One was "Draft Board Theology" and the other was "Revolution 1976," both of which appeared in* Commonweal *and both of which were very striking. I had seen them that summer of 1967 and I went back to them in the fall and was really persuaded that something was terribly wrong here.*

In the fall of 1967 I was teaching in St. Louis Providence Junior High School, and I decided that I should make some small effort to protest what was happening in Vietnam and so this is when I started sending back my draft card. I sent back a total of four draft cards to the federal folks and they finally drafted me in March of 1968.

I went back and read what I had written. (He was wrong; the two articles he named had not been reprinted in A Theology for Radical Politics *but they had appeared in* Commonweal.) *My words were: "It is time, I think, for many older persons to rebel. Unless many of us are willing to go to jail, too many of our best youths will go. 'Realism' and 'working in the system' are no longer enough; the cost has become too high."*

While David was free on bail and awaiting appeal, on October 30, 1969, he was driving near Omaha with several other Brothers when their car skidded into a truck. The car burst into flames. David died, with two of his Brothers.

His friend Brother Joseph Forgue later frightened me again:

You might be interested, by the way [he wrote in a note on other business], in learning that what David and Basil were going to do on that ill-fated visit was to discuss your "Human First . . ." chapter from A Theology for Radical Politics *and an essay of Sam Keen's. Ditto copies of both were littered at the wreck site.*

Sometimes as I write, I see images of that burning automobile and the strewn copies of my work, and the flames darting from the basket at Catonsville.

There are many ways of giving witness.

Introduction

The lifeblood of English and American philosophy has for centuries been its involvement with the daily life of ordinary people, its preference for ordinary language, its insistence upon verification in the concrete contexts of daily life. (Contrast the abstractness of Continental, especially German, speculation.) It is not surprising, then, that readers have responded with perception and critical acumen to *A Theology for Radical Politics*. Above all, I appreciate their quickness to grasp its central point: that the location of theology is not in the conceptual mind only, but in the imagination, the passions, the body, and the social reality in which and through which the person makes his real assents.[1]

The main argument of that book did not take the form of logic or conceptual analysis, although such tools were used where necessary. The main argument of that book was made by way of constructing fresh images by which a Christian sensibility and Christian experience could be focused upon a new set of intellectual and political problems. Images are more than half of theology (and philosophy). If you get the fundamental metaphors right, the rest of the analysis is *comparatively* easy and accurate. If you work with the wrong model, metaphor, point of view—if your imagination approaches the data wrong —brilliant technical analyses are of little avail. H. Richard Niebuhr states this point as follows:

What is the general idea in such interpretation of ourselves as *symbolic* more than as *rational* animals? It is, I believe, this: that we are far more image-making and image-using creatures than we usually think our-

[1] John Henry Newman, *An Essay in Aid of A Grammar of Assent* (New York, 1955), especially Ch. 4, "Notional and Real Assents."

selves to be and, further, that our processes of perception and conception, of organizing and understanding the signs that come to us in our dialogue with the circumambient world, are guided and formed by images in our minds.[2]

Getting the imagination straight: a primary axiom of sound theology.

A second axiom of sound theology: *Every key theological word acquires its concrete meaning from the social and political context in which it is used.*

"Despair" means something different to a pregnant black woman on the South Side of Chicago and to an unhappy housewife in Lake Forest; "hope," "freedom," "love," "justice," and other key words also have quite a different contextual ring in different locations. *Who* is using a given theological word? From *which* social class and historical tradition? In *what* social context? With *what* repercussions for the political situation? The task of our generation is *to bring theology to political consciousness.* Our teachers these past three generations brought it to historical consciousness.

To bring theology to political consciousness is not to "politicize" theology, or to make it less than transcendent in its scope. I hate the word "relevance." If it is true that I have always[3] tried to keep my theological work in constant and complex involvement with political and cultural affairs, it is from a motive quite the opposite of a concern for fads. I have no hesitation about taking unpopular or untimely views; I move at my own momentum and pace. But at every new theoretical step it has been my habit to ask: How would that distinction, or insight, or analysis, affect decisions taken by government or cultural agencies today? A systematic thinker should be prepared to turn his equipment in many different directions, as daily life demands.

---

2 *The Responsible Self: An Essay in Christian Moral Philosophy* (New York, 1963), pp. 151–152.

3 As far back as I can remember in my schooling—even in a parochial grammar school—I have edited or written for a paper whose aim was to unite "religion and culture." We had good priests in our many parishes and intelligent nuns, who encouraged me in both directions. I'm not sure they're happy with what turned out—but their early help made a certain outlook second nature to me.

I am in complete agreement with Peter Berger's observation in *Movement and Revolution* [4] that most of the important events in one's life are not directly political, and that to reduce life to politics is to diminish it grotesquely. I am further in agreement with him that theology is about God, about a dimension of life that is sacred and transcendent to our ordinary doing and thinking.[5] But every theological statement has, I hold, an experiential base and a political, cultural context. To speak of God is to speak from a politico-cultural location, to look in a direction, to recommend attitudes and actions whose implications have a political dimension. Those who think theologically must become aware of the political context in which their words acquire significance; those who act politically must be aware of the dimension of the sacred which transcends their efforts.

Politics is, in a sense, a world of illusions: of shifting symbols, priorities, sentiments, alliances; of unplanned consequences, dashed hopes, shattered certainties, sudden rescues; of organized spontaneity, and chaos under a veneer of bureaucracy. It is only barely and unreliably a field for the sort of reason that works by generalization. It is, on the other hand, a field of difficult responsibility and hard, unevadable tasks by which man works out his destiny, and either builds up or devastates the world. Politics, not a merely private life, has become the arena in which men wrestle for their salvation.

That salvation concerns not only their personal integrity, their souls, but also the fate of the race. The conflicts and complications are many: good men supporting destructive causes, untrustworthy men supporting life and growth. Politics generates irony, tragedy, and sometimes comedy. To say that man is a political animal is to say that politics is man.

That is why politics is of such deep interest to the theologian. "Building the Kingdom" is a political task. Grace comes to the political animal. What we mean by "God" is highly conditioned

4 With Richard J. Neuhaus (New York, 1970), p. 13.
5 Peter L. Berger, *A Rumor of Angels: Modern Society and the Rediscovery of the Supernatural* (New York, 1969), p. 2. See also his excellent piece, "A Sociological View of the Secularization of Theology," *Journal for the Scientific Study of Religion*, VI, 1 (Spring 1967), pp. 3–16.

by our political location, direction, self-criticism. And, in any case, the concrete world of this present history is where we who are living look for the living presence of God—not elsewhere, not only to the past, not only to the future. It is in humble things that God characteristically shows himself. "Shows himself"? We do not see God. He does not reveal himself directly. But we have been tutored by the image, story, and sense of reality of Jesus—who, being God, chose not to try to become everything, infinite, universal, but ordinary flesh in one place at one time; and who emptied himself of pretension, accepting the irony and tragedy of death and failure as the ordinary path by which significance, other-centered love, and historical fruitfulness are sown. And thus we try to discern in the politics around us on which side we should throw our weight; with whom agree; with whom disagree.

Often we wrestle darkly, in a polar night. Aware that our most serious political judgments may be in error, we live by Augustine's maxim: "In necessary things, unity; in doubtful things, liberty; in all things, charity." That political judgments are characteristically doubtful is all the more reason for voicing them explicitly and publicly. Our hope as a human community for arriving at anything like an approximation of the truth arises from the criticisms we make of one another's judgments. There is no possible way to arrive at an "objective" direct view of reality. What we can do is create such a context of intelligence and mutual criticism that the perceptions and final judgments of each of us are shaped by the contributions of all the others. Political judgment is a social acquisition.

Moreover, much is to be gained from studying theological judgments in a concrete context. Where does a man get the "story" that he thinks human life—his own, his nation's, the world—is living out? Where does he get his image of community? What does he take a human person to be? What connections does he see between primitive and archaic and modern man? With which segments of human history does he identify for his sources of illumination and his criteria of judgment? How does his "sense of reality"—what he counts as real, im-

12

portant, meaningful, worthy of attention—express itself in the complexities of concrete experience? What are the contours of his imagination and passions—his favorite metaphors, his enthusiasms?

Theology is in large measure the study of "intelligent subjectivity," [6] and of personal and communal "standpoints" [7]— the study of "alternative visions of personal identity and human community." [8] For our always inadequate image of God is based on who we think man is: based on our understanding of personal integrity and human community. If we think integrity is a matter of obeying laws, God tends to be imagined as lawgiver; if we think integrity is a matter of honesty, God tends to be imagined as the source of that inner light by which we judge ourselves; and so forth. All through our lives we hear "rumors of angels," but as, through suffering, we grow more and more into "the stature and wisdom of Jesus Christ," we form a sharper and sharper sense of reality in communion with his: we "put on the mind and heart of Christ," until "he, not I, lives in me." We make his story our own.

Critics of *A Theology for Radical Politics* tend to overlook the theory of standpoint and image on which it was built. They fail to notice that every key image (personal identity, community, wisdom-in-action, being ["Beautiful, man!"], hope, evil, idolatry, freedom as appropriation, the Legend of the Pure Protester, Mediterranean man, honesty, community, the Oneness of everything, and so forth) was ancient and Christian; it was not a "new" but an "ancient" theology. It was, even, specifically Catholic in its symbolic emphases: on creation rather than redemption, on nature rather than history, on the deficiencies and dangers of enthusiasm, on the love for fleshly things and a suspicion of a too prophetic, too spiritual, outlook. When Norman Mailer coined the word "hip" which was to become "hippie," he understood that the cultural complementarity

[6] See my *Belief and Unbelief* (New York, 1965), pp. 16–17.
[7] See my "What Is Theology's Standpoint?" *Theology Today* (April 1968), pp. 37–51.
[8] See my *A Theology for Radical Politics* (New York, 1969), p. 20, 30–46.

"Catholic-Protestant" helped to clarify that between "hip-square." [9] The shift in Harvey Cox's thought between *The Secular City* [10] and *The Feast of Fools* [11] was mediated in a crucial way by his sojourn in Catholic (and even in primitive) Mexico.

Few noticed, either, the way in which my analysis of "the tyrannical majority" (Chapter 4)—which diverged from the then popular "power elite" theories of the new left—was later confirmed by experience under the Nixon-Agnew administration. And a number of my colleagues wrote to me of their confusion about where I am going. Perhaps a few notes on how I locate myself among my fellow theologians will help.

Young men are fortunate when in the generation charged with instructing them there are unquestionable giants. Those of us in religious studies have been singularly blessed. There have been astonishingly great human beings in our field during our youth. Many of these men—Mircea Eliade, Teilhard de Chardin, Karl Barth, Romano Guardini, Karl Rahner, Martin Buber, Gabriel Marcel—have helped to shape who we now are. But there are three whose lives and work have been especially dear to me: Reinhold Niebuhr, Bernard Lonergan, Paul Tillich. It is impossible to do all that those men did. Yet one wants to let their light be reflected in all one does, as appropriate gratitude for what they did for us.

I scarcely knew Tillich: a lunch, two conversations, an evening together at Harvard (I introduced him and Gustav Weigel in the first public ecumenical discussion in Sanders Theater). I have met Niebuhr only once, for an hour's walk and tea one summer afternoon in Massachusetts. I took one large public course and one seminar under Lonergan in Rome, and see him all too briefly from year to year for fleeting but rewarding conversations.

[9] *Advertisements for Myself* (New York, 1959), p. 379.
[10] New York, 1965.
[11] Cambridge, 1969. See my "The Secular City as Fantasy and Festivity: Response to James Hitchcock," *Journal of Ecumenical Studies*, VI, 2 (Spring 1969).

Most of the influence of these men upon me, in short, has been in the silence of my room as I sat studying their books, often with fiercely awakened passion. Books are an unparalleled form of communication, intimate, exact, rich: like sending long letters, full of detail and revelation, to one's beloved. My best friends in life, I sometimes think, I have met through books. Even with those friends whose face-to-face companionship brings subtle, poignant, and rich joy, it is often books that have woven the network of bonds between us about which we do not need to speak.

There is one other model I should mention, far more important in my early years, a figure whose true range and power was not felt (I discover) by many outside the Catholic community: Jacques Maritain. Maritain is perhaps the most gentle and saintly of my teachers, the most profound in his understanding of prayer, contemplation, poetry, the silences of beauty. I remember the burning of my heart, which actually was so painful that I had to set the book aside many times and walk outdoors, when as a college sophomore I read, and re-read, *Creative Intuition in Art and Poetry*.[12] I believe that that book cured me once and for all of the tyranny of words, of the worship of analytic concepts and mechanical rigor. It focused my attention upon the fruits of the pre-conscious workings of the intelligence, and upon the living act of insight whose expression, whether in concepts or in works of art, never equals the original splendor. Maritain's zest for politics, culture, prayer, the arts, as well as for the heights of theoretical inquiry in philosophy and theology, communicated itself to me. *True Humanism*[13] became a model for what I wanted to conceive, and my thirst to acquire sensitivities and skills along as much of the "range of reason" as I had talent and energy to absorb borrowed its fledgling shapes from the beauty of Maritain's own life and writings.

No one who knows the work of Bernard Lonergan will fail to recognize how much, on every page of my work, I have been influenced by distinctions, turns of mind, and systematic inter-

[12] New York, 1955, especially Ch. 3, "The Preconscious Life of the Intellect."
[13] New York, 1938.

15

ests of his.[14] It is probably true that among some Lonerganians I am not regarded as an orthodox interpreter; it is certainly true that the momentum of my intellectual life always was, and remains, my own. But just as in my college years I took Maritain as the teacher I trusted most to shape my mind, because of his charity, his huge cultural range, his concreteness, his love for theory for its own sake, and his prophetic depth, so also in graduate school (such long, lean, painful but, in retrospect, fruitful years) I entrusted the formative "set" of my mind to Lonergan as to no other thinker. I did so because Lonergan is not a conceptualist. He focused my attention where I wanted it to be: through my own subjectivity towards liberation. His interest in and knowledge of politics, the arts, and concrete life in general disappointed me; but the strength of his analytic tools was enormous because of their flexibility and adaptability. His basic standpoint is self-revising, self-reflective, self-critical. In learning from Lonergan I did not have to become captive of his vocabulary, his way of doing things, his directions. I got clear in my own mind what *my* experiences have been, *my* insights, *my* judgments, *my* actions, and what through those operations of mine seemed communicable to others. I learned a style of analysis that is applicable in any field in which experience, understanding, judging, and deciding operate. In a word, I could take up Maritain's cultural range without the directly scholastic vocabulary; I could use Lonergan as a springboard towards a vocabulary that was of our century, in the English language, in a secular idiom, with a carefully guarded and experiential opening to the transcendent.[15]

Tillich's romantic temper, deeply Platonist and Germanic, held a fascination for me; temperamentally I am inclined in similar directions. But my early love for Aristotle and early years of much meditation upon the fleshy concreteness and limitation implied by the incarnation of God in history set me the task of countering those inclinations. Thus, what I liked best

14 Especially his *Insight: A Study of Human Understanding* (New York, 1956), and *Collection* (New York, 1967).
15 I state my differences more clearly in "The Lonergan Explosion," *Commonweal* (May 29, 1970), pp. 268–270.

in Tillich were those occasions on which he overcame his romantic, ecstatic side: the existentialist, concrete side of his thought. What I liked least was the (it seemed to me) too firm and too confident planting of his feet in the standpoint of the Enlightenment combined with that of "the Protestant principle." There was a kind of moralism in his thought, manifested most clearly in *Christianity and Its Encounter with the World Religions,*[16] in which Christianity appeared too much committed to changing history, to moral responsibility, to head and conscience and individualism. I preferred those moments in which Tillich expressed a deeper sense of unity with God and nature, a contemplative and social and less alienated soul; and in which he recognized God as "the depth dimension" of all things, always and not merely in ecstatic and revelatory "moments." The cult of moments has always seemed to me a sign of weakness, a loss of daily and constant connectedness, a sort of romantic reaching to escape this good, concrete world. At some later time, I would like to spell out these differences in greater and systematic detail. In any case, Tillich reinforced, often in a stronger and deeper way, the longing for systematic thinking and a holistic cultural perspective that Maritain had first awakened in me.

In graduate school, I believe I read virtually every word that Reinhold Niebuhr ever wrote. I went systematically through *The Christian Century* and *Christianity and Crisis,* as well as through every other periodical I could trace and obtain. What I loved best about him was not only his contact with daily events, his taste for politics and social analysis, and not even the fact (which in terrible, dark moments gave me a thin ray of hope) that he had never earned a doctorate, but above all his deeply Greek sense of irony and tragedy. The Greek spirit has always been my starting point, a touchstone, a refuge for my soul; I cultivate those pagan roots. In Niebuhr—whose *The Irony of American History*[17] was the first volume to come into my

[16] New York, 1963. By contrast I especially like *The Future of Religions,* edited by Jerald C. Brauer (New York, 1966), *The Courage to Be* (New Haven, 1952), and *The Dynamics of Faith* (New York, 1965).
[17] New York, 1952.

hands—I felt instinctive trust: a man in touch with earth, with man, with bitterness. The writing of almost monthly columns on political and cultural events was a learning device of his whose fruits I saw in his life's work, and decided to make my own. My interests are more epistemological, more systematic than his, however; and in the debates between him and Tillich I mainly took Tillich's side, except that Lonergan's methods seemed to me more empirical and flexible than those available to Tillich from his beloved Schelling and Hegel.[18] I also have a stronger sense of community than Niebuhr, except for *Man's Nature and His Communities*.[19]

A few briefer words on some of my contemporaries. What I most admire in Thomas J. J. Altizer is his profound, romantic opposition to the "red-toothed Reason" of the rationalists. With Blake, he sees Satan in every form of manipulative reason. His touchstone figures—Dostoevsky, Nietzsche, and Hegel—also loved that dark side of Greek consciousness I wish to nourish in myself. But Altizer gives "modern consciousness"[20] a much more normative weight than I wish to give it; he also defines that consciousness idiosyncratically, with scarcely a reference to the dominant cultural forms of pragmatism, linguistic analysis, empiricism. He treats "reason" in far too undifferentiated a way. And he writes almost entirely from the perspective of the head and the alienated ego; his dominant concerns are with intellectual traditions and movements. Thus he writes of the vision of hell in Nietzsche, Blake, and others, but not of Auschwitz. There is very little social, political, or economic consciousness apparent in his analysis of human identity. He is unusually selective in his borrowing from Christian symbols—the redemption is archaic, but the cross is almost everything; descent into hell, but no ascent into heaven. The force of his "radicalism" is, I think, individualistic, alienating, and not "revolutionary" (as he calls it). It offers us more of what already is suffocating us

18 See "Paul Tillich," in my *A Time to Build* (New York, 1967), pp. 232–265.
19 New York, 1965. See my "Moral Society and Immoral Man," *ibid.*, pp. 354–372.
20 See especially, *The Descent Into Hell: A Study of the Radical Reversal of the Christian Consciousness* (New York, 1970).

18

to death. I share his disdain for certain kinds of rationalism, tradition, alienation; I part company when, instead of seeking a new viewpoint, he reacts in the direction of romanticism.

What I admire most in Harvey Cox is his sense of responsibility as a pastor, and his alertness to the importance of basic metaphors and images of life. He refuses to write what would merely please the professionals; probably no theologian more gets under the skin of his colleagues, and accepts himself and his role courageously in the face of constant slights. My instincts are more metaphysical and systematic than his, and I want to work out an underlying standpoint that looks in many directions at once; Cox, it seems, is more fearful that such speculative interests are untimely, impossible nowadays, and not germane to the pressing, desperate needs of many struggling people. By altering the moral connotations surrounding words like "secular" and "city," Cox deeply stirred the psychic and imaginative life of countless of his readers. By questioning in *The Feast of Fools* the "profane" and "pragmatic" consciousness he had earlier celebrated, he moved many yet another step in a series of personal conversions. I would like to develop a theory of "intelligent subjectivity," "conversion," "standpoint"; for the experiential base of the perennial sense of the sacred and the transcendent resides in such experiences. I trust the German sense of history and the future far less than Cox; and respond much more to the Mediterranean sense of nature, the ontological sense, the sense of the sacred, than he.

Two other visions of contemporary theology may be mentioned; both are rooted in the world view of the contemporary university. Martin Marty is an historian of religion, and while he makes constant and regular comment on political and cultural events, he takes an approach far different from mine.[21]

[21] See *The Modern Schism: Three Paths to the Secular* (New York, 1969), but especially, "Liberals—Not Radicals—Will Rebuild the University," *National Catholic Reporter* (April 1, 1970), p. 6. Marty notices my shift in "mood" viz-à-viz the youth culture. He also notes that I still have not re-embraced liberalism. Then he suggests: "Wouldn't he and we all serve the cause more if we stressed the pluralism, the amplitude, the potential for self-criticism, the syncretistic embrace, the openness of many elements in the liberal humanist community—rather than engage in sadomasochistic lumping of 'our crowd' with its worst."

Marty writes with a detachment and astringency that are classically "Enlightened," with a confidence in reason, civility, and, in general, liberal humanism which I do not share. He is not, I think, able sufficiently to unmask the mythical structure of the liberal's "objectivity," nor to trace the lines of power and corruption therein. He stands much more than I with that part of the university traditions whose genesis is in the Enlightenment. Consequently, on some battles we are on the same side; on others, we are opposed. Objectivity, clarity, analysis, and the like seem to be normative for him; "intelligent subjectivity" operates in that role for me.

James Gustafson is an ethicist of great analytic power and technical skill. Where Marty is historical, Gustafson is analytic and systematic.[22] He tends to take the work of others and "get

---

The qualities Marty lists are admirable ones, and the more they are cherished and practiced, the better. Still, the image for intelligence from which he operates—openness in the marketplace of ideas—is not sufficiently inventive, creative, or personal to do what intelligence must do today. I would like to keep the qualities he lists, but add other ones made possible by a new image for intelligence. That is what all my work is about. Instead of stressing what is right with enlightened liberalism, I would rather try to help invent a new form of intelligence.

[22] See, for example, "Ethical Theory and Moral Practice," *The Christian Century* (December 17, 1969), pp. 1613–1617; "New Directions in Moral Theology," *Commonweal* (February 23, 1968), pp. 617–623; and "Christian Faith and Moral Action," *The Christian Century* (November 3, 1965). Gustafson's work has shifted the ground of ethical discussion in two major ways. First, he notes that the debate between a "principle ethic" and a "situation ethic" cannot be won by either side; each says something valuable. See "Context vs. Principles: A Misplaced Debate in Christian Ethics," Marty and Peerman, eds., *New Theology 3* (New York, 1966), pp. 69–102. Secondly, he notices that ethical claims by various authors must each be understood from "the point of view of the author," and he identifies his point of view as follows: ". . . the key terms used are not drawn from revelation, or even from theological literature. This is done out of the conviction that any significance of the work of Christ for the moral life takes place through such aspects of selfhood as disposition, intention, and judgment that are common to all men." He adds that he has not yet "developed systematically all the aspects of my understanding of man as moral actor, as responder and initiator in a socio-historical process." See his introduction, "A Study in Ethics: A Statement of Procedure and Method," in *Christ and the Moral Life* (New York, 1968), pp. 8–10. His conclusion, in chapter seven, "A Constructive Statement," calls attention to perspective or fundamental angle of vision and posture of life; attitudes and dispositions; fundamental intentions, purposes, and ends; and norms. My own categories (sense of reality, stories, symbols, principles, and facts) are not far distant. But Gustafson's are worked out in closer connection with systems of con-

clear about it," "sort things out," "make distinctions," "line things up." His rigor, care, thoroughness, and clarity are qualities I deeply admire. Still, my memories of the competence and precision of the scholastic philosophy which was my first intellectual context make me skeptical about choosing that set of values and criteria for myself. Many must do so if we are to get anywhere. But there is another order and range of tasks which must also be done. Besides conceptual clarity, there is also clarity about the images, stories, and sense of reality which place concepts in a concrete context and give them their concrete bearing. There are the problems of personal ethical growth and development, and of cultural and political criticism. And there is, finally, the creation of a new model of intellectual inquiry, better adapted to the clarification of the role of the imagination, nonverbal perception and communication, goals, hopes, and values than the model of conceptual rigor and precise verbal statement. Ethics is only in small part the realm of principles and logic; it is chiefly the realm of stories and the dialectical move from conversion to conversion. It is for that reason, I think, that academic ethical studies today, despite their high polish, seem less than adequate to the task of speaking well and clearly about daily ethical realities.

The following essays on concrete ethical problems make clearer, for better or worse, what I have so far been able to do with the new standpoint, new method, and new approach that I have been trying to work out. It is, in a sense, an ancient standpoint, method, and approach—more like the *"phronesis"* of Aristotle, the *"sapientia"* of Aquinas, the "illative sense" of Newman, than like modern "science" or "analysis." It involves attention to metaphor, image, story, sensibility, and sense of reality, as well as attention to "facts," rules, norms, concepts,

ceptual clarification, and I wish to work mine out more in the context of concrete politics, social analysis, and personal awareness. He shows that objectivity is a form of what I call "intelligent subjectivity"; and in a sense I begin where he leaves off. The self must risk asserting itself in order to create, not in pride but in humble charity; Gustafson, however, may in his caution be heeding H. Richard Niebuhr's sharp warnings against "self-defense," "the most prevalent source of error in all thinking and perhaps especially in theology and ethics." See *The Meaning of Revelation* (New York, 1967), p. x.

and analysis. The specific theological content is most often conveyed through metaphor, story, sense of reality than through explicit conceptual statement. It would be an easy enough task to abstract out such conceptual materials. But that would render ethical analysis more like logical analysis, and thereby leave out almost everything that is distinctive about the way people actually act and what action signifies. To express in a fuller way the theoretical underpinnings of what I am doing is the systematic project in which I am engaged, while practicing the art regularly in such work as the following.

I hope students in particular find as much fun in thinking about these essays as I had in writing them. I would be glad to hear from them about their reactions. The material under inquiry, after all, concerns events in the first years of their maturing political and theological consciousness: materials as searing in the memory as their first loves, their first betrayals.

Bayville, New York

The Burden
of American Morality

1. Desertion

PARIS is hauntingly lovely in October. The small-leafed trees lay the scents of their dying on the brisk air; the centuries-old bricks and roofs grow mellow in the thin autumn light. The thick, grey Seine is sluggish; the printsellers stamp their feet impatiently. If one has to choose exile, what other city promises similar intelligence, conflict, and delight?

In the last week of an October, we went to Paris, a dozen of us under the sponsorship of Clergy and Laymen Concerned about Vietnam, to visit the deserters from the United States forces, and to talk to the North Vietnamese, the National Liberation Front, and the United States mission. An aide to the American ambassador rejected our request for an interview; the North Vietnamese were cordial and friendly, but cautious, towards a rump delegation of five from our number; the representatives of the N.L.F. met nearly all of us in their newly opened Paris office; and nearly twenty of the American deserters living in or near Paris came to see us during receptions at our hotel. In the streets outside, fascist and left-wing students, in the ancient tradition of Parisian student activism, took turns bombing one another's restaurants, bookstores, and presses (there were at least five separate bombings during the two nights of our stay).

We learned little from the North Vietnamese, except their desire that the American people should hear *their* interpretation of the war as well as Washington's interpretation. They could not imagine how anyone believes that the Vietnamese, North or South, can be considered "aggressors" in their own nation, or how anyone can fail to see that the United States is a distant, white, foreign nation. "Peace with honor" was just as valuable to them as to Americans, but the solution which seemed honorable to the North Vietnamese was quite different from any that Americans had been prepared to face. The North Vietnamese delegates were warm, sensitive, intelligent men, who spoke willingly about the friendly relations that might one day obtain between their people and the American people—once the unfortunate decisions of recent years had been repudiated by the American government.

The representatives of the N.L.F. were outwardly cordial but emotionally and intellectually uptight. They were none too warm in their references to the North Vietnamese; the warmest they could get was to support the North Vietnamese demand for a bombing halt. Beyond that, they seemed to say, *they* and not the North Vietnamese are the interested party in further negotiations. The men of the N.L.F. were as intransigent and rigid as human beings can be. We were perhaps the first, or very nearly the first, delegation they had met in their new office, a modest fourth-floor apartment in a middle-class Paris suburb. They seemed nervous and afraid; they consulted frequently, and seemed to disagree somewhat among themselves, but with the harder line coming out victorious every time.

They also seemed afraid that the North Vietnamese would, once again, betray them to their enemies and enter upon negotiations that would benefit the North at the expense of the South. They were insistent (a) that the N.L.F. *is* the legitimate government of South Vietnam and (b) that the N.L.F. is *already* a "coalition" government. They showed no signs of willingness to compromise with the present Saigon government of President Thieu. They spoke of him with contempt, insisting that without the Americans his regime would not last twenty-four hours. They were not interested even in discussing the "neutralist alliance" which they announced with so much fanfare during the Tet offensive. Their line was much more intransigent: the Front already represents a broad national alliance. They admitted there were Communists in the Front but could not estimate their number or influence; they were amused by such a typically American line of questioning. They pointed out that none of the four present (including the translator) is a Communist, or has ever worked with a Communist in the Front.

I noted that Truong Dinh Dzu, the peace candidate imprisoned under the Thieu regime, had taken a step in the direction of the Front by advocating a coalition government to which they, as individuals, could be admitted; would they take any steps in his direction? Their reply was that the future is entirely up to Mr. Dzu; he could embrace their program in its entirety, otherwise he was of no interest to them. In brief, the position of the N.L.F. outlined to us in two hours of intensive questioning was the most uncompromising, intransigent, and demanding they had enunciated at any time during the war. Whether this intransigence represented their vastly improved military position —since Tet they controlled nearly the entire countryside, free even of search and destroy operations—or whether it represented a caution and harshness appropriate for the opening round of negotiations I could not determine. Clearly it would be much easier to deal with the North Vietnamese than with the dissidents in the South. (The fact that the Saigon government was just as intransigent as the N.L.F. suggested the character of the war: an internecine Southern civil war, in which both sides have entrapped their relatively unwilling allies.)

Our main task, however, was to speak to the deserters. The group in Paris seemed at ease and relatively happy: Paris excited most of them. The French government required new work permits every fifteen days, unless they found permanent employment; their insecurity, therefore, was great, particularly since employment was exceedingly difficult to find in France, and in Paris especially. The twenty young men we talked to in Paris— handsome, bright, articulate—knew of perhaps ten more deserters who were not present, and thought there might be two or three score others, unknown to them, in various provincial cities. All of them needed money, and most desired a stronger sense of community among themselves; but some, like the guitarmaker who found a job in Marseille, a gentle and solitary young man from a small town in Montana, were content to do their work alone and in peace.

In Stockholm it began to grow dark at 3 o'clock in the afternoon; the countryside was a dull winter brown; and the Swedes, prosperous and formal, did not smile. There were at least one hundred fifty deserters in Sweden still, even though perhaps thirty others found the task too difficult and the blandishments of U.S. agents too compelling and returned. Sweden has long had probably the most effective and enlightened program for political refugees in the world, and accepts the young Americans under the category of those who flee for "humanitarian" reasons. Some eighty-four percent of the Swedish people opposed the war in Vietnam, and of those many publicly accused the United States of unjust aims and unjust means of warfare, and thought of the North Vietnamese as heroic in resisting our vast firepower in the name of Vietnamese independence. Still, young men who desert the armed forces of their own country could not expect an entirely sympathetic reception. Particularly since the Russian invasion of Czechoslovakia, cold war memories had returned to Sweden and public opinion was less certain than it had been concerning the deserters. Moreover, the Swedes were extraordinarily middle-class and prosperous; what use would most of them have for young men who did not yet speak Swedish, who had not found solid, permanent income, and who lived off the pittance assigned them by public welfare? Even the beautiful, free Swedish girls of the movies seemed to be, in real life, forbidding and quietly calculating; they were liberated, and no romance or first experience with sex was liable to sweep them off their feet and make them forget the difficulties of the future. In Sweden, the official welcome was generous and many Swedes were willing to help; but the climate was rather bleak.

Most of the eighty or ninety young men we talked to in Sweden, like most of those in France, came from the South or the Midwest; few had had even a year or two in college; many enlisted at seventeen or were drafted at eighteen. They were unusually bright and alert; they did not talk, as one World War II veteran in our group put it, "like we used to talk in my four years in the army." We were warned that most of these young men were lower middle-class, and might not be as articulate as the college students we were used to. It was true that, as a rule, the deserters had not read much and did not have full and round theories about their action or about the United States; but they expressed their feelings and ideas eagerly and well. They seemed to be from among the brightest of those who are unschooled. Although in the small towns from which most of them came they had no tradition for examining and questioning American political life, and particularly American foreign policy, they were acute enough to see through the army and its propaganda. (Their experiences suggested that someone should submit himself to the army preparation for troops leaving for Vietnam, and report on the view of the war presented by the army.) Several told me that they were first alerted to the lies and untruths of the war by veterans returning from Vietnam. I didn't find a single deserter (although there must have been some) who even realized, before his desertion, that there was a large theory-oriented peace movement or who had read any of the books critical of the war. Their resistance to the war grew out of their own guts, in confrontation with the army; only afterwards did most discover books, theories, and reasons.

The young men we met compared favorably to college students who seek counseling on the draft: penetrating, sensitive; only they were not rich enough, or bookish enough, to be in college when the army called. To accept induction was the easy, natural path of the conformity and docility which it is the business of American grammar schools and high schools to teach them: not critical, not questioning. Almost all of those who spoke to me were not pacifists; they were not absolutely against war, or the army; except for the peculiar nature of the Vietnamese war, a war on the poor, on civilians, in support of a vastly unpopular Saigon government, they would have still been in the army, getting their term of duty over with. What were two quick years in the army compared with a lifetime of exile? They chose the harder and more difficult course, for which growing up in America had not prepared them.

One member of our group, from Des Moines, was the mother of one of the boys: a little heavy, sweet-faced, good-humored, she told us later that her son had not changed at all, "Just like he always was." He told me that he was proud of her coming; she had always taught him not to worry about what other people thought, and to do what he thought was right. He looked like a young boy in a Shakespeare play: long black hair, tight orange corduroy ski pants, dark boots, a heavy blue sweater. One could not help admiring the strength it took, given the patriotic propaganda and pressures of the Middle West, to come from Des Moines to Stockholm.

Some of the young men imagined that some day in the future people would appreciate the courage their action required, and they might become national heroes—men willing to endure being called villains. They were buoyed by the numbers of men who continued to swell their ranks, and by the huge number of A.W.O.L.'s the army—particularly on the West Coast—had to cope with. Some felt guilty for not staying in the army and waking more of their buddies up. One handed us a letter to the American people in which he begged them to "wake up from your sleep," so that he could again be free to return to the land he loved. He saw his desertion as an attempt to get at least a few people to think about what America is doing to itself by this war.

The United States government, for its part, worked in many open and covert ways to sow dissension among the deserters and in the Swedish government, and to persuade the deserters to quit. A nation founded by political refugees (my own grandfather fled Czechoslovakia to escape the Austro-Hungarian draft) is embarrassed when the refugees go the other way. Our delegation was in Stockholm too briefly, but several thought we saw quite clearly the hand of undercover agents, urging an extremist left-wing line that would discredit and divide the deserters, and leading sharp personal attacks on the one man in the Swedish government more than any other who had championed the young Americans. The Swedish people, meanwhile, did not experientially understand that many Americans saw the war as a matter of moral, not only political, conscience, and hence they did not understand the degree of moral conflict felt by young men who, when they did what they had decided they ought to do, were branded as deserters and traitors. The cross currents of emotional guilt and confusion whipped some of the young Americans back and forth. They badly needed a young Christian minister in Stockholm, who could help them with their many problems, lead them in seminars about American society, and represent them before respectable Swedish people. (In Paris, the group had just such a minister, and he was highly effective.)

On the other hand, many of us felt humbled; we had written against the war, but we did not face the choice of carrying arms in it or going to jail. We saw the political foolishness and moral outrage, but we were not forced into exile. Our consciences were formed easily. These young men carried the cruel burden. It may be true that some of the more gentle and freer of them would have deserted in any war; certainly virtually all of them found the army a brutalizing assault on their dignity as human beings. Their witness, however, was primarily that they were lower middle-class, not college-educated, not pseudo-intellectuals. The parents of many of them, they said, were voting for George Wallace. These very decent boys wanted the United States out of Vietnam, and they wanted to come home. They deserved amnesty: they, with their buddies in the field, have carried our guilt long enough alone.

2. Voluntary Service in Vietnam

A RED-BEARDED Australian ambulance driver was the first to alert me to the crisis in the ranks of the American voluntary agencies in Vietnam. A volunteer himself, he was in Hong Kong for a two-week rest. He told me that personnel in these agencies would be among the best to talk to for a clear view of what was going on in South Vietnam, during the month of August 1967.

"They don't see with military eyes," he said. He further explained that the voluntary agencies "cover a spectrum," from the hawkish to the dovish. He placed the Catholic Relief Service "pretty close" to one end of the spectrum, and the American Friends Service Committee "pretty close" to the other. (The meaning of "hawkish" and "dovish" in this context, he made clear, means willingness to be identified with one side in a military-political struggle.) This conversation was to be repeated to me many times during the next month.

There are twenty-two voluntary agencies in South Vietnam, of which seventeen employ American personnel. Of the total of three hundred Americans working for these agencies, one hundred seventeen work for International Voluntary Services (I.V.S.). The next largest group, with fifty-three Americans, is Vietnam Christian Service (V.N.C.S.), the combined Protestant effort in Vietnam, administered by the Mennonites. It was these two groups, "left of center" in the terms defined above, that were undergoing the greatest strain, but especially I.V.S.

The director of I.V.S., Don Luce, was a soft-spoken, granite-willed Vermonter, now in his thirties, who had been in Vietnam for over nine years and intended, one way or the other, "to spend the rest of my life here." Mr. Luce was an expert in agricultural research, as were many of his fellow workers. Together with thirty-seven Vietnamese and six Filipinos, the Americans in I.V.S. maintained homes in almost fifty towns in thirty-four of South Vietnam's forty-four provinces. Many worked with refugees, some were specialists in community development; others taught agricultural theory and techniques, elementary science, or English; and others worked with Vietnamese youth.

In all the frustrations of their difficult assignment, many I.V.S.'ers had over the years learned to rely on the imperturbability and calmness of Mr. Luce, as well as on the good humor and gregariousness of Mr. Gene Stoltzfus, an ordained Mennonite minister and expert in community development. Stoltzfus was the assistant director of I.V.S. and had been in Vietnam since June 1963. The shock to I.V.S., then, when Messrs. Luce and Stoltzfus tendered their resignations, as a protest against the U.S. policy in Vietnam, was little short of fundamental. (By the time they released the news to the press, two other Vietnam staff members had joined them in resigning.)

Neither Luce nor Stoltzfus were of the dramatic type; both were reluctant and cautious protesters. "I'm a professional in community development," Mr. Stoltzfus explained. "How can I develop community when it is U.S. policy to destroy community?" Mr. Luce spoke quietly and clearly: "I feel that if I had said something publicly two or three years ago, maybe some of these things wouldn't have become official policy. For a long time I thought that it was my job to build quietly, no matter what others did, so that at least some people would be building. But I was wrong. Now it is impossible to do anything —even what we do is being used to help justify what we can't approve."

Almost thirty other I.V.S. personnel prepared a statement, which would go out to other members in the provinces. Two weeks later, fifty had signed a statement to be sent to President Johnson. The first draft hardly hides the smoldering passion:

In the past, I.V.S. has made claims to political neutrality. Such claims are no longer tenable. We see ourselves being used in Vietnam and in the States to sell the validity of the U.S. position in this country. In Vietnam I.V.S. has become increasingly involved in the Pacification Program. In the States public officials and the press cite I.V.S.'s presence in Vietnam, cite *our* work in Vietnam, as a testimony to the essential benevolence of the American intervention.

But this is not the testimony we want to make. Some of us would have preferred to remain neutral and quiet. But **our** neutrality has already been violated. We're moved to set the record straight and then to take what steps are necessary to get back where we started from, working with people because they're people, not because they're potential dissidents from American policy.

The proposed statement went on to list some of the events I.V.S. personnel had observed, the policies they had watched develop and the feelings they had seen grow among many Vietnamese. Unlike the U.S. military, I.V.S. personnel remain in Vietnam for at least two years, and many stay longer, especially those who are professional in their field. Again unlike the military, all the I.V.S. workers learn Vietnamese. And most unlike the military, the I.V.S.'ers live with, eat with, and talk with the people.

I had a chance to read through I.V.S. files for the last few years: the regular familiar reports from the field, private letters, and folksy newsletters meant for friends and associates. A complicated, many-sided view of the war emerged from them, as it did from the hundreds of conversations I had with I.V.S. personnel in their central headquarters in Saigon and in the field. Characteristically, the man or woman in I.V.S. is not a protester or a demonstrator; he is an individualist, trying to work within accepted structures at his own pace and in his own way. Most are silent, independent, determined persons, able to live virtually alone for long stretches of time, without the books, music, and conversation to which they are accustomed—all are highly educated. It is not always easy for a stranger to strike up a conversation with an I.V.S.'er, even at dinner at the I.V.S. house. The dominant image I received of the I.V.S. "type"—it is not a good one, but it comes to mind insistently— is that of the quiet man of the range, the Marlboro man.

Most had felt the security situation worsen in the last two years. Towns, villages, and hamlets that once had been safe were now the scenes of small-arms fire at night, mortarings, the early morning danger from mines, and at least partial overrunning—as happened at province capitals like Tuy Hoa (where all Americans had to be evacuated) and Quang Ngai. (Tuy Hoa is the capital of Phu Yen Province, one of the two provinces in which, General Westmoreland was fond of claiming, pacification had made most progress.) Many will tell you of hamlets they no longer are welcome in, or of homes in which they once would have been happily invited to tea, but in which Americans are no longer willingly received.

Some I.V.S.'ers have watched American troops participate in the questioning of "suspected V.C." (In many areas, all Vietnamese are "suspected V.C.," but some are a little more so.) On one occasion, the suspect was blindfolded and put in a helicopter that then took off; after several moments of hovering only three feet from the ground, the blindfolded man was shoved out to what he thought was his death. On another, blindfolded men were made to run full-tilt down a hillside; at the bottom strands of barbed wire had been strung. Then, bleeding but still blindfolded, they were made to run down another hill, without barbed wire.

"We don't accuse the American soldiers of deliberate cruelty," the I.V.S. working paper said. "Perhaps if you accept the war, all else can be explained." In any case, it isn't the small-scale incident that is weakening the fabric of Vietnamese culture and the structure of her social life. It is the large-scale American strategy: "the free-strike zones, the refugees, the spraying of herbicides on crops, the napalm."

At lunch one day with the Quakers, I heard unusually loud bomb bursts. "We'll be busy later this afternoon," one of the nurses at the civilian hospital commented to her companion, without interrupting the flow of conversation. The bombing, we later discovered, was about four kilometers outside Quang Ngai city,[1] in a region where there is nothing but hamlet next to hamlet, rice field to rice field. Something had been spotted there.

[1] Within a mile or two of the famous My Lai IV.

In some sectors there, civilians had been warned to move out because the V.C. were known to be strong in the area. "If they stay, they're V.C.," I was assured by an authoritative American official. "They simply have to learn that if they place their bets on the losing side they will pay the price. I don't have much sympathy for them. I didn't have much sympathy for German civilians under the Nazis."

More striking to the agricultural experts in I.V.S. is the direct effect of herbicides on their work. One worker, who wrote his master's thesis on the herbicide 2-4D, carried a petition from farmers in his area to a colonel of the First Cavalry Division, begging the Americans to desist. Many farmers had to replant their crops; all reported lower yields; weaknesses were developing in the plant strain, making it both more vulnerable to new diseases and less fruitful.

High winds often forced the C-123's to fly higher than controlled spraying permits, and the same high winds carried the spray great distances. Moreover, a much stronger concentrate than necessary was commonly used for faster and more certain results.

The colonel replied by trying to have the I.V.S.'er reprimanded officially, and by telling the farmers that the V.C. had stolen some herbicide and "must be shooting it down from the mountains." At An Khe in April 1966, an I.V.S.'er wrote, farmers complained repeatedly to the First Cavalry Division that they were losing nearly their entire crop, and that it was risky to invest in a crop there and too costly to lose a single one. The military did not seem to understand.

Perhaps enough has been written elsewhere about the American strategy of making refugees to indicate what the I.V.S. personnel see. Quang Ngai province has a population of 700,000; the number of refugees has passed 160,000 and will move towards 200,000 by the end of the year. In the nation as a whole, two million of fifteen million have become refugees; some of these have been moved as often as four times. The young men are usually placed in interrogation camps; few are seen with the refugees. The number of pregnant women (among other signs) suggests, however, that a certain number of absentee husbands are hiding out nearby, presumably with the **V.C.**, now more highly motivated.

Vivacious people, at ease, happy (*vui*) in an active and energetic way, Gene Stoltzfus explained, the Vietnamese, more than any other people, want to love the Americans. Confused in their attempts to govern themselves, bitterly divided, having lost precious leadership through years of unenlightened French politics and brutal civil war, many Vietnamese at first looked to Americans with hope and friendliness. Their reaction now can be expressed in one word, Stoltzfus and his friends believe: disappointment. The American way of making war is destroying their rice fields, their hamlets, their people. They asked for help, not for all that technology. "The answer to a sniper's rifle-shot is not a bomb," a Vietnamese major exclaimed passionately to one American.

But even the American presence, Don Luce insisted, is disruptive of Vietnamese culture and mores. I.V.S. has found it increasingly hard to find suitable homes to rent for its female participants. "It's hard to find places not near a brothel," Luce explained. "Vietnamese families become very upset when Americans move near."

Often, middle-class Vietnamese families have to move to poorer areas, unable to compete with the inflation caused by the multiplication of Americans, and obliged to rent out their homes to make ends meet. (Speculators and landowners, of course, are making immense profits.) "Very little money goes into productive industries," Luce explained sadly. "The quickest way to make money is in brothels, bars, hotels, restaurants —services for the Americans."

What were I.V.S.'s plans for the future? Luce, Stoltzfus, and a core of others wanted to launch a truly international voluntary service, drawing upon volunteers from all nations and working in every nation. They felt they could not work conscientiously in South Vietnam without also sending help to North Vietnam, or in Saigon-controlled areas without also helping V.C.-controlled areas; the problems of development do not have national boundaries. They regretted very much their dependence on the Agency for International Development (A.I.D.), and thus on the State Department. Whatever neutrality they had tried to maintain collapsed as the military assumed tighter and tighter control over all aspects of the American presence in Vietnam. Moreover, new pressures were felt almost every month. Military officers and high-ranking civilians alike used the word "treason" in describing certain I.V.S.'ers—one of whom continued to teach English at the University of Hue, despite the American effort to punish the University after the struggle movement of 1966; another of whom protested the war in a letter published in a national journal back home.

"We want the normal civil rights of American citizens," Don Luce insisted. But since it didn't seem possible to have such rights in Vietnam, and since American strategy did not seem to include the concerns of the Vietnamese people, I.V.S. was about to lose its most outstanding and experienced members, and perhaps to give birth to a new instrument of international civilization. Such a rebirth would be extremely difficult. Where would the funds come from? But even its possibility lent some hope to these words uttered to an I.V.S.'er by an old Vietnamese woman in a refugee village: "These sad days are filled with napalm, hate, death. The rice fields turn brown. The new year makes me afraid."

3. Vietnam at Peace

A CONVICTION is growing among thoughtful persons in the Peace movement that the political settlement of the war, which now seems inevitable, will not be easy. Travellers abroad, even behind the Iron Curtain, report that the American withdrawal might be as precipitate and unwise as President Johnson's escalation, and that, in human terms, the last stage may be worse than the first. The criticisms have even gone so far as to suggest that the Peace movement is in the immoral and impolitic position of demanding a settlement whose human costs will be extreme. Every outcry by the Peace movement, the argument runs, now has a different political effect from formerly. Earlier, the movement succeeded in convincing Johnson, and then Nixon, that a political settlement must be made. Now the movement gives indiscriminate negotiating leverage to North Vietnam and the National Liberation Front—whose designs on Vietnam's future are neither wholly popular nor notably humanistic.

The Peace movement has neither need nor time for self-doubts. It is still crucial to press a not exactly over-eager Nixon. However, at least the more intelligent and critical wings of the movement will want to begin thinking of a more morally and politically valid concept than immediate withdrawal. As the political aim of a movement, the cry for immediate withdrawal is simple and powerful. As a policy that can and ought to be effected, it is sadly deficient.

During my brief thirty-day tour of South Vietnam during the elections of 1967, I spoke often and at great length with Truong Dinh Dzu, who was later imprisoned, and then I tried out his ideas on other South Vietnamese leaders like Premier Huong, as well as against my own experiences. My long conversations with

Dzu firmly fixed eight or nine points in my mind. Now that the unreality of other approaches to peace has become evident, such points may also persuade others—both by their inherent plausibility, and by their respect for the complexities of Vietnamese culture.

I. *Many South Vietnamese are passionately opposed to the National Liberation Front.* By now, many thousands of families have had at least one person whose hand has been cut off, or whose life has been taken, through Viet Cong terror. Many persons say with deep feeling: "If the Viet Cong come to power, *we* will go into the hills." Independently of the military, of Thieu-Ky, or of Catholicism, there is strong resistance against the Front in Vietnam. The depth of that feeling surprised me.

II. *The primary source of political strength for the N.L.F., and also of its political unity, has become hatred of the condescending American mission.* "We are caught," a Catholic refugee from the North told me, "between a hammer and an anvil: the Front and the Americans." He was on the brink of joining the Viet Cong. He spoke of the millions of refugees from American operations, the squalor of the swollen cities, the defoliation of the best agricultural areas (along roads and streams), and the degradation of many thousands of Vietnamese families, whose women were bought for the consumer goods of the half-million Americans replacing one another in rotation year after year. The Americans will all be gone in seven or eight years, I told him. "Eight years will be too late," he said heatedly "My daughter is ten years old." The next night, a friend of mine attended a party which turned into a farewell for three students of Saigon University, who were slipping off that night to join the V.C. (and who expected, like many raw recruits in the guerrilla army, to be dead before too many months).

The overwhelming American presence gives the V.C. a unifying political issue they would not otherwise have. American trucks go through Vietnamese villages at thirty miles an hour (to go slower in some areas would be dangerous) and thin clouds of dust penetrate the bamboo houses; women hold cloth to children's noses. Wherever the Americans go, bombing and strafing aircraft arrive. Viet Cong militancy rises. Americans mean death. "The Front," Mr. Dzu explained to me, "faces the same difficulties as all political groups in South Vietnam. We have never been a nation. Each group is loyal to itself and fears the others. Delta people do not trust Northerners [that is, north of Saigon], those in Central Vietnam do not respect Southerners. Catholics, Buddhists, Hoa Hao, Cao Dai; mountain people, farmers, city people—South Vietnam is a land of many dialects, many political conflicts. When the Americans leave, the Front must make deals with every local group. They must become pragmatic like everybody else."

III. *After the hostilities stop, there will be a crucial, uncertain period of three to five years.* The National Liberation Front is unquestionably the best nationally organized political body in South Vietnam; and it is the only group, outside A.R.V.N., that is armed. Still, the ranks of its elite veterans have been decimated by the last five years of savage fighting; the number of times the most courageous front-line officers and elite demolition teams go into battle without dying is not infinite. Thus it is by no means certain that the Viet Cong could militarily overrun South Vietnam within three to five years after a large-scale American withdrawal. On the other hand, it seems highly probable that in five to ten years the Front would dominate South Vietnamese politics. It will have talent, organization, the prestige of having fought off the Japanese, the French, and then the Americans—and its own independent army. Everything depends (1) on the national prestige and quality of the chief opposing political parties; (2) on whether it or the Front will be better able to unite the many factions of Vietnamese politics; and, (3) on the political role of the South Vietnamese army.

IV. *During this critical period, there is danger of large-scale reprisals against political enemies, from both sides.* The Thieu-Ky regime is as capable as any of the assassination, torture, or imprisonment of political enemies. A friend of mine working in one village told me of Viet Cong soldiers interrogating two women in the field and shooting the one whose husband was an A.R.V.N. soldier. Vietnam has a history of savage civil war. Meanwhile, the three or four million Vietnamese who are working for the Americans or in other ways directly implicated in

41

the American presence are more compromised than those who, fifteen years ago, worked for the French; and some cities have large cemetery plots commemorating the thousands murdered by the Viet Minh when hostilities ceased in 1954. Some sort of internationally supervised guarantees must be agreed to and enforced.[1]

V. *An American withdrawal will have to be phased and as many as fifty-thousand men will have to be left in Vietnam for three to five years.* Economically, the transferral to Vietnamese management of the huge airbases, communications centers, and other facilities constructed by the Americans will require time. Both the North Vietnamese and the Americans have some stake in overseeing in some minimal way the protection of the people their presence compromised. And a sudden disorderly withdrawal of American forces from regions which both economically and militarily almost wholly depend on them would be as grievous as our initial buildup; like getting a girl pregnant and then abandoning her. The phased American withdrawal will require a public timetable, faithfully observed. The first 300,000 men should be withdrawn quickly.

VI. *The corrupt Thieu-Ky regime is the fundamental obstacle to stability after an American withdrawal.* The regime has been, even accounting for the immense American superstructure, more stable than seemed possible in 1966. Still, it is no match, politically speaking, for the N.L.F. In the elections of 1967, almost half of those of voting age (in Viet Cong or disputed areas) did not vote, and of those who did only thirty-one percent voted for Thieu-Ky. Such a weak vote is startling, since more than two million persons of voting age depend directly on the Thieu-Ky regime for their office and livelihood: soldiers, officials, wives, and closest relatives. No issue during the "thirty days of free speech" (election of 1967) aroused crowds more enthu-

[1] Vietnamese frequently replied to my questions about a bloodbath: "But how could more be killed than today, every day, by Americans?" The number assassinated by the Viet Minh in 1954 was grossly exaggerated by Western propaganda. See D. Gareth Porter and Len E. Ackland, "Vietnam: The Bloodbath Argument," *The Christian Century* (November 5, 1969), pp. 1414–1417; Tran van Dinh, "Fear of a Bloodbath," *The New Republic* (December 6, 1969), pp. 11–14; Frances Fitzgerald, "Vietnam: The Future," *The New York Review of Books* (March 26, 1970), pp. 2–10.

siastically than comparisons of the regime with that of Diem, and even Hitler. The Buddhists, especially, hate the regime. "The junta would not last one day if the Americans did not enforce it," I was told many times. "If you would even look the other way, down it would come." On the other hand, towering political leadership in South Vietnam is not in abundance; and control over the loyalty of the army is a crucial condition for political leadership. Mr. Dzu, for example, has the backing of important Hoa Hao, Cao Dai, and Buddhist officers; but could he hold the loyalties of the dominating Catholic officers? It did not hurt one's advancement in the French army or administration to be Catholic.

VII. *It makes neither political nor economic sense to imagine Vietnam permanently divided in two (like Korea and Germany).* Traditionally, the industrial and educational energy of Vietnam came from the North, its rich agricultural culture from the South. The university center has been Hanoi. Even today school children in Saigon, asked to name the capital of Vietnam, reply "Hanoi." In Mr. Dzu's opinion, fifteen years of separation between the two parts of Vietnam, North and South, (never intended as a *political* division, but as a temporary *military* truce line) will require an equivalent period of time for reunification. It was part of his election platform to promote a series of solidly designed actions, both national and international, to bring North and South Vietnamese into consultation, cooperation, and gradual, mutual organization. Economic aid, for example, could in some cases be distributed through joint planning commissions. Representation at the United Nations and elsewhere should gradually become cooperative. (Many North and South Vietnamese of Mr. Dzu's generation went to school together in Hanoi, have intermarried, or are related by blood.)

VIII. *The form of economic life in a United Vietnam will probably be some combination of government planning and free planning.* Some of Vietnam's problems of geography and resources—regarding transport, for example—cry out for social control. The massive problems of the new sprawling cities created by the war in the South will not yield to uncoordinated free enterprise. On the boundary lines between Chinese collectivism and the capitalist sphere of Japan, Vietnam might be expected to try to bend both worlds to meet its own peculiar problems.

IX. *The main task of the U.S. in bringing about peace is to lower the threshold of military firepower and military operations, to put into effect a U.S. cease-fire, and to let the onus of destruction fall on the Vietnamese.* It is not likely that, either politically or militarily, the North Vietnamese and the V.C. can happily afford to continue hostilities at the present high level; it is not likely, either, that they will capitulate at the present level. In the name of their own future, neither North nor South Vietnam has anything to gain by further bloodshed and technological destruction. It is probably true, both Mr. Dzu and Premier Huong agreed in 1967, that the U.S. build-up prevented a victory of the N.L.F. in 1965. But the American strategy thereafter was increasingly self-defeating. Military and American priorities were given precedence over political and Vietnamese priorities. The Front grew dramatically, even as its military units had to depend more and more on North Vietnamese replacements.

Mr. Kissinger's argument for two-way peace talks—U.S. and North Vietnam; South Vietnam and N.L.F.—is faulty for two reasons. In the long run, North Vietnam and South Vietnam must reunite; culturally, economically, and politically, unity makes more sense than division. Secondly, in order to withdraw its troops according to a publicly announced timetable, the United States does not *need* a previous agreement with North Vietnam. Three considerations support this point: (a) The Americans don't need all the personnel they have in Vietnam; the numbers, in fact, are counterproductive. (b) The North Vietnamese have *domestic* reasons for lessening their efforts in the South and *international* reasons for not wishing to become further dependent on either China or Russia; and they have shown evidence of willingness to keep infiltration rates low and to withdraw units from fighting. They will not, of course, abandon their Southern compatriots while the Americans remain there, nor cease at least periodical offensive operations while the Americans launch them without pause. (c) The

North Vietnamese have little reason to trust the mere words of Westerners, by whose solemn treaties they have been repeatedly betrayed. They have suggested they will respond in kind to American *actions*. Americans outnumber North Vietnamese in South Vietnam 5-1. We could remove 100,000 men and watch for them to withdraw 20,000. Such actions speak louder than talk in Paris.

X. *There is no need, then, for Americans to await verbal agreements in Paris.* The chief American tasks are three: (1) to cease offensive operations and bombings; (2) to begin withdrawing troops according to a public timetable; and (3) to make plain in word and deed that the interests of the United States do not require Thieu and Ky as the heads of government in South Vietnam. A nationalist regime in South Vietnam, close to the Buddhists rather than to the minority Catholic army officers, has a slim possibility of surviving the American withdrawal during the three- to five-year critical period of uncertainty. The Thieu-Ky regime has no such possibility, as they themselves recognize.

By its large-scale presence in Vietnam since 1965, the Americans have given a Vietnamese "third force" a chance to catch its breath and to identify its interests. By Americanizing and militarizing the struggle, the Americans have almost generated their own defeat by polarizing the issue between Thieu-Ky (who in fighting for the French fought against their own people) and the N.L.F. Thieu and Ky seem themselves often ashamed, for the symbols that surround them were first French and now American, but not Vietnamese. It is time now to yield Vietnam back to the Vietnamese, in an orderly way that does not compound the damage we have already done the culture and the flesh of that people, and that wrests from what we have done there some at least of the high aims we have all too often publicly announced.

The Legacy
of Revolution

4. The American Revolution: 1976

THERE was never any doubt whose city we were in. The first billboard at O'Hara field was emblazoned with the name. The same name, in a signature as childlike as a nun's, met the visitor in the windows of restaurants; it was blocked out on hotel marquees and imprinted on yellow cards under telephone receivers. We came to Chicago to indulge the ego of Richard J. Daley. For five years we had been indulging the ego of Lyndon B. Johnson. The good of the people, the good of the party, had become secondary.

The thin dry fumes of the airport bus soured the cool autumn air. Driving into the city was like entering Barcelona in 1956, or Paris during the Algerian terror, or East Berlin: policemen on the corners, in hotel lobbies, on the bridges over the expressways. We entered a city with its disguises down, a city founded on the bedrock power, not of persuasion, but of gun and club. It would be a rhetorical mistake to say that we encountered fascism in Chicago, but we saw something very close to it: an American form of undemocratic power, brazenly displayed. Worse, the people love their own disease. In the packed galleries the last night, hastily printed orange placards announced a people's love for the local strong man. Telephone calls and letters to Chicago papers ran ten-to-one in favor of the tyrant and his police. A hasty national poll found that seventy percent of the population favored the Daley policies. Two days after the convention Hubert Humphrey succumbed yet again and supported Daley as he had long supported Johnson. The love of tyranny is a national disease.

What we learned in Chicago is that America is not yet a democratic country, has not been one, and does not wish to be.

For what happened in Chicago is not new in America. There were bloody draft riots in 1863 and in every war until 1941; there were cruel steel, coal, and farm riots in the 1930's, bitterly suppressed by mounted police who did not scruple to fire their guns into the crowds; political conventions have often before been cheaply staged and rigged. By comparison, the shocking events of 1968 were even mild. What was new was television, with its educated and urbane and resourceful newsmen; it was not by accident that strong men like Daley and Wallace singled out newsmen as agitators, for the perspective brought by newsmen was not that of simpletons or local flunkies. What was new was also the steadily growing proportion of the educated population, now almost thirty percent of the voters. What we saw in Chicago was the drama of a new class warfare.

There is good evidence that the Humphreys, Muriel explicitly, saw the 15,000 students chanting their disaffection in the streets merely as a nuisance, a blemish, a disagreeable stench upon the sweet winds of fulfilled ambition. There was no sign that those in charge of the convention or the majority that selected Humphrey understood the depth and extent of the disaffected class. Their explanations of what was taking place around them revealed the limits of their understanding: Eugene McCarthy was a victim of personal pique; the ragged radical young were assassins, terrorists, and communists; the "clean for Gene" kids were only a step from becoming hippies; the hippies were profane, dirty, lazy perverts; the convention minority was moralistic, pious, and disloyal to the party. Not long after the brutal beatings outside the Conrad Hilton hotel I heard two well-dressed women express their shock, not at the bloodshed, but at the profanity the young radicals had used, words these two women had surely heard before and surely used. The affluent Texans and the tough, hardworking, plainly dressed salesmen and farmers and lawyers who made up the party majority espoused views and cheered lines almost indistinguishable from those espoused and cheered by the plusher Republicans at Miami Beach.

By all reports, Miami Beach exuded an air of unreality: yachts and lavish dinner parties and stunning party dress, against the distant backdrop of racial war. Chicago was closer to the tensions that divide our country: lower-middle class, meaner, tougher. What was startling was that the affluent suburbanites represented by the Republicans and the tough little people and establishment politicians represented by the Democrats now had the same interests: *preserve* America upon its present course, *maintain* the present law and order, *unite* to cover over our divisions. Ironically, the new left had handed both Republicans and Democrats a target around which to unify: the confrontation politics of the poor, the black, and the proponents of peace in Vietnam. Republicans and the Democratic majority were lining up together against the disturbers of the status quo. The reality so painfully clear to the new left was utterly invisible to the great majority of Americans. There was almost no possibility of communication between the two visions of reality, and the differences were too deep for a pragmatic consensus or compromise. Since views of reality are socially enforced, we may expect a new era of systematic silence. Thus America has already entered a "get tough" phase, to which presidential candidates must cater.

It was enough in Chicago to wear a beard or long hair, to be young, to have a McCarthy button, to carry a camera, in order to be subject to intimidation. The electronic machines at the International Amphitheater and the omnipresent police created an atmosphere of uncertainty and randomness; one never knew who would be searched or stopped, or why. The police were brusque and rude, as befits their class; to cry injustice or to struggle was to resist arrest. The sense of fear was eerie and tangible. At Grant and Lincoln Parks one never knew when the surrounding police would strike, how violently, or why.

Those who boast how much they love America (businessmen who sing a patriotic hymn at every weekly luncheon) are closing ranks against those who love their nation for its achievement of justice, but hate its injustices. For many, loyalty is the highest virtue; God is an American, or wishes that he were; and it is inconceivable that basic policies of our nation might be immoral or unjust. Thus the meaningful and fundamental struggle revealed by events in Chicago is between those who hold irreconcilable views about what is actually happening in America, between those who think American institutions are sound and adequate and those who judge them harshly: between "good people" and "agitators." The meaningless struggle was between Humphrey and Nixon for the right to represent the boosters.

At the moment when the machinery of the convention, abetted by majority sentiment, was inexorably electing Hubert Humphrey as its candidate, I stood near the circle of young people seated in Grant Park and ringed by soldiers and barbed-wired jeeps. The young people listened to passionate speakers—Norman Mailer was there, Monique Truong (the daughter of Truong Dinh Dzu), delegates from the convention, and speakers of their own. The crowd responded spontaneously to almost every sentence: jeers, laughter, agreement, applause, anger, objection. Every so often another hymn was sung, of justice and peace and solidarity and resistance. The measureless cruelty of four hours earlier had risen to its climax and passed, leaving a kind of peace, a fatigue, a surcease in its wake. Under the dark swaying trees, one could not help thinking of prayer meetings and itinerant preachers; the young were not acting apart from American traditions. Many clean McCarthy kids and newspapermen and well-dressed staff workers had joined the meeting. Near me three observers, quite clearly not participants, turned away to speak to one another. In my dark suit and tie I looked enough like a secret service agent to follow them each time they moved and I stayed constantly within earshot. They became visibly annoyed and found occasion to jostle me to determine whether I had a gun; and then they followed me to find out who I was.

We are back, I thought, where we began: October 16 in Oakland, October 21 at the Pentagon. Once more the blue-helmeted, paunchy police, the pink-faced guardsmen who would rather be hearing rock, the desperate anger and hopelessness and desire of the young. Eugene McCarthy had tried for nine months to provide the young with one last attempt at electoral politics. And we were back where we began. Dick Gregory told the students that there was hope the voting age will be lowered to eighteen. They jeered: *"Vote? Who for?"*

In Chicago, leaders of the demonstrations had asked permission to use Wrigley Field, Comiskey Park, Soldier's Field, and every meeting hall they could think of. Mayor Daley refused. The young were allowed nothing but the streets, no walls but officers and troops. (Would Mayor Lindsay have gone to chat with them, sent them doughnuts and coffee, helped them set up tents?) The right to free assembly? The right to voice grievances? The sympathy and assistance due the young? The young have concluded that the only effective political tactic in our society is confrontation. The young, not the delegates of the minority in the convention, unmasked Mayor Daley, just as earlier they had set fire to Eugene McCarthy and toppled Lyndon Johnson; just as now they would "Dump the Hump!"

The institutions of American democracy have been allowed to stagnate for so long that substantive issues cannot be raised; first, procedures must be changed. Between 1964 and 1968, the Mississippi and Georgia delegations were enabled to take an important step, procedurally. In 1968, the unit rule was eliminated. In four years, that procedural change, too, will bear political fruit. But in that four years, a great many of the young will be called to die for policies they morally abhor.

Still, despite the urgency and the desperation, an armed revolution is not an open option. A society overprotected by police, guardsmen, federal troops, and technological devices is so strong that a revolution like that of 1776 is no longer possible by force of arms. It is frightening to think that revolutions can no longer occur; that we are trapped. Hence the desperation of the young. On the one side, the logic of confrontation demands that, ultimately, the young will have to meet the police not with unprotected heads but with rifles and grenades and terrorism; but the logic of taking up arms against the United States is the logic of fruitless defeat. On the other side, electoral politics seems so illusory that the young do not understand the naïveté of those who take it seriously. What, then, can be done?

The overriding fact was that the Democratic Party adopted a Republican position in Chicago, and it was absolutely clear that the young did not represent a majority of Americans, even in the Democratic Party. One might wish to argue that the primaries and the polls showed that the Democratic machinery was not representative of a majority in the party who wanted serious change. (Johnson will go down in history as the man who led the party from its highest peak to its lowest depth in four nasty, short, and brutish years.) But this argument fails to note the inroads of George Wallace in traditional Democratic areas, specifically areas in which Robert Kennedy was strong. For the distress of poorly educated whites, who are caught between unattainable affluence and the menacing advance of the poor, is undifferentiated. It could be led in any of several directions. As McCarthy himself admitted in Oregon, this forgotten class voted for Kennedy, not for McCarthy. Now that Kennedy was dead, there was no intelligent and liberal leader to hold their trust, no one but Wallace. Between the radical young and the seething lower-middle class—between the young and the cops—there was no understanding, no yet discovered bond.

Armed revolution will be crushed; the only way to a revolution in America is through the slow, cumbersome, long march of the ballot box. A new party must be built, but it will not be built at once. Four steps seem to me necessary. First, efforts heretofore virtually non-existent (except for those of Robert Kennedy) must be launched to reach and to lead the class from which cops, cab drivers, and millions of others come. This is the major, indispensable task of a new democracy. It is this class that supports Mayor Daley and always is tempted by a strong man; in Germany, it supported Hitler enthusiastically. It responds to the gut feeling that it is not forgotten, and that its interests are being cared for; it seeks a father.

Secondly, advantage must be taken of the defeat of Humphrey and, with him, of some Democratic regulars, so that a new Democratic party may be fashioned on the ashes of the old. The strong minority at the convention already forms a major base. Bright, young suburban voters of liberal bent provide an extensive voting public; it was the genius of McCarthy to be the first to discern their strength and build a "new politics" upon their numbers.

Thirdly, a way must be found to unite the liberal wing of the Republican party to the new Democratic party. For interest-group politics in the United States is losing its rigidity; new divisions and new cohesive bonds are being shaped along the lines of political, intellectual orientation. It is not exactly ideology that is at stake, but it is bent of mind and attitude; it is a different approach to and perception of reality. The growing mood of "toughness" threatens liberal Republicans and liberal Democrats alike.

Fourth, a decision must be reached on whether to abandon the Democratic Party or to make it the vehicle of radical change. The formation of a new party will require much more time than the renovation of the existing one. Moreover, the danger of sectarian zeal and exclusiveness is especially great in the movement to a new party. Alienation from the rest of American society is likely to be heightened and the real political power of the left is not likely to be appreciably increased. On the other hand, there were no viable alternatives within the existing structures in 1968. A vote for Humphrey and his supporters was intolerable. An actual vote for Nixon (however much one wanted to see the defeat of Humphrey, as the only hope for building a new party) called for self-abnegation beyond the claims of duty. Not to vote at all was, of course, to refuse to give either Humphrey or Nixon a "mandate." The developing alternatives since 1968 appear little more promising. But how, then, shall we channel our political energies?

We may imagine a strategy aimed at 1972 and 1976, consisting of at least five steps. (1) Develop new leadership throughout the Democratic Party, in every town, county, and state. (2) Support candidates of the new politics, Republican or Democrat. (3) Seek to bring Democrats and Republicans of liberal bent into common organizations. (4) Continue the radicalization of liberals and begin to struggle for a new realism among radicals— a new political synthesis. (5) Devise strategies and seek candidates who appeal to and lead the lower-middle class.

A revolution is a long-term affair. The young accomplished more in 1968 than anyone could have predicted. They prompted a more radical realignment in American politics than has been experienced for more than thirty years. They found Eugene McCarthy, who was willing to personify and politicize the vagrant despair and hope they felt in 1967. The fact that McCarthy fell short of the presidency, and even of a peace platform, reminds us that miracles are not often granted, and that revolutions usually demand many long marches, many defeats, many dry seasons, before they yield success. The young, like many in the last two centuries before them, will grow up in a revolutionary struggle and, when it succeeds, will be its seasoned leaders. Until then, there is no alternative but the patient guerrilla warfare of unromantic and difficult ward politics, united fronts, and unremitting concentration upon the goal: an America worthy in 1976 of 1776.

5. Why Wallace?

ANDY RESTEK runs the Texaco station in a Pennsylvania steel town. His brother Pete works in the mills. His other brother Steve, I think, is a manager at the local Sears or some other chain. In any case, all three Restek brothers voted for Wallace. Why? And why do they hate the hippies so much, and praise the Chicago cops?

Andy Restek has two kids in college—one at State College, and one at the local branch of the University of Pittsburgh. He wipes the grease from his hands as he talks about them, and pushes back his heavy rimless glasses. He is rather proud that his children will all go to college—and a little ashamed to say that he is glad they won't be gas station attendants. He envisages Bob as a clerk in a bank (as he is, summers) and later as an officer; Bob's a pretty bright and impressive boy, with personality and presence. He hopes Sally will marry a nice, solid fellow with sound ideas. Since Andy's parents came to America with nothing, he's rather passionately uncritical about the nation. He has a fairly comfortable house and nice lawn, a new Plymouth, and the youngest boy is a much touted junior halfback.

Andy served in Italy in 1944-45, and has served as an officer in the local V.F.W. He knows he has worked hard, and has succeeded. He lives in a better neighborhood than where he began, and he owns the station. He's been a good mechanic and has a lot of loyal customers. The neighborhood where his station is located, however, is run-down and the ugly houses that are not unoccupied (windows broken, doors boarded up) are inhabited by passive, silent blacks. There is no need to rehearse Andy's attitudes to blacks. "I'm no racist or bigot; it's only that . . ." From that point onward he merely reports the evidence of his own senses, as his perception shapes that evidence: dirty, passive, strange, unreliable, careless. Andy points out that Harry Scott, the black man who works at the Esso station seven blocks away, has what it takes; he works hard, which only shows they can do it if they want, and proves that Andy isn't prejudiced. It's the majority of Negroes who are lazy that cause the trouble. Andy doesn't see any difference between the starting place of any black man and his own starting place. The only difference he perceives is one of initiative and brains.

Andy responded to Wallace, I suspect, because Wallace put things exactly in the way Andy's experience has put them. Andy doesn't understand sociological or psychological or economic theories. But he catches the tone in which all those people on television or in the papers talk about such things. They don't say that they're out to destroy sound family values, or common sense, or tough, hard work and painfully acquired respectability. Educated people talk with a kind of code. They try to sound harmless, but you know they're trying to take your world from you. You can almost feel them screwing you; you see it in their complacent eyes. They know so much.

Andy trusts his own experience. He knows what he knows. And he likes his world, his home, his America.

He is very worried about Sally. He saw a picture of a long-haired boy in her wallet and threw her out of the house for several hours. He doesn't dare allow himself to think that she has been taking pot, but sometimes his stomach tightens. He tries to get her to cut her long hair and not to wear it straight, and hates when she merely tells him he's old-fashioned or doesn't respect his word as law. He blames himself for working too hard—American materialism, his pastor would say—and not being as strict with her as his parents had been with him. She would *never* have talked back to them that way. She hates church so much, and refuses to go to confession, that he knows there is trouble brewing. If she gets pregnant . . . he can't allow himself to think that, and strikes out in fury at every manifestation of the kind of youth he despises: shiftless, dirty, uninhibited, smart-alecky, superior, aiding our enemies.

The outrage he feels is so deep he can't understand how any-one in his right mind would not scream out in anguish at what is happening to America. He wants authority to tighten up, in part to assuage his own guilt for having been too soft with his kids.

He watches with trepidation the books that Bob brings home. Bob is majoring in business administration and finance. But Andy is suspicious of some of the poetry and novels he brings home, and books with words like "humanism" on the jacket. In Andy's experience, "humanism" has been one of the code words for soft-headed thinking, pornography, and the collapse of authority.

Andy's brothers Pete and Steve largely agree. They grow bitter often when they get together. Their wives hate to hear them begin to talk politics. Even miniskirts—much as the men joke about them man-to-man—have become for them one more symbol of the collapse of values. And Hollywood and television and the liberal reporters. The hometown newspaper is solidly conservative; but the lurid ads for the movies still announce the general sickness. It's just like the priests say. Secularism is the collapse of all decency and morals and au-thority. We need a man who talks sense and isn't softheaded about authority, to clean this country up from coast to coast. That way, we can all have the America we worked so hard to build, which gave us what success we have.

Andy, Pete, and Steve are all for the underprivileged, but (they say) let them prove themselves by work, the way we did. "Racism" and "bigot," they have come to think, are other code words by which the white-handed, effeminate Harvard men want to call the good people evil, and win the allegiance of the blacks for their own political and unstated purposes.

6. The Politics of the Seventies

THE most important political task of the coming decade is to tap the energies of the men and women of the lower-middle class: gas station attendants, firemen, policemen, storekeepers, millworkers, low-budget salesmen, local "rednecks." Possibly a third of adult Americans spring from this class. Only now are large numbers of its young people going to college—often "apathetically," resistant to the culture of the universities. The American military draws a disproportionate share of its manpower from this class, both through the draft and through recruiting campaigns. More than any other, this class foots the emotional-psychic bill for the decision, made by others, to allow the black, brown, and red man to get a fair share of white opportunity. This class feels helpless before the liberal-conservative coalition that manages American society. Although many of its members voted for Humphrey in 1968, many were tempted sorely by Wallace's observation: "There isn't a dime's worth of difference between Republicans and Democrats." It is a class ill-prepared to understand either international or national politics; its loyalties, traditions, and patterns of judgment are local.

The experiences and sentiments of the lower-middle class are thus increasingly opposed to the abstract, national ideals of American liberalism. When liberalism was the champion of shorter working hours, higher pay, the right to strike, and social security, this class was content to invoke a national, even international, idealism over against the entrenched, hereditary opposition of local establishments. But under the impact of the technological explosion since World War II, the social and political situation of the lower-middle class has been altered dramatically. Liberalism has become increasingly the property of the technical, educated middle class. That new class is committed to the rationalization of society, work, and urban living, and caught in the inner contradiction between affluence based on the technology of war and its own ideology of reason, law, tolerance, and order. Formerly, the lower-middle class was opposed by a conservative, landed class of owners; now it is opposed by a liberal, educated class of managers. Its older opponents kept its members from control over their destiny by economic privilege; its new opponents keep them from similar control by technical expertise. The old system was plutocratic, the new one is meritocratic. Both leave a very large class feeling increasingly helpless.

There are many ironies in the present situation of the lower-middle class. Its members face a whipsaw. On the one hand, the conservative, established classes regard them as uneducated, rough, uncouth, unreasonable in their demands for higher wages and security, and dumb. On the other hand, the liberal educated classes regard them as naïve, prejudiced, rigid, superstitious, requiring much missionary effort before they can be considered genuinely human. When radical students call them "pigs," the pain surely penetrates. The conservative classes do not find their manners or their morals adequately stable; yet the standards of dress, speech, and public decorum they manage, with great effort, to impose upon themselves are mocked by television writers, academics, intellectuals, artists, some clergymen, and some segments of the press. They feel looked down upon because their manners are untaught; and then they witness the sons and daughters of the privileged violating with impunity every inhibition they themselves have been forced to nurture. Disciplined in sexual conduct, hygiene, docility, and obliged to acquire a cooperative, competitive spirit, they are now told by radicals that the price they paid dehumanized them—and by conservatives that our whole civilization depends upon paying that price, ever more rigorously.

They are exhorted to return to God, and to forget him; to renounce their concern for money and a higher standard of living (their "materialism" and "secularism") and to act upon their own interests more realistically. They are urged to be

61

patriotic and to "support our boys in Vietnam"; and, imagining themselves to be Germans under Hitler, to stop the war. They are beseeched to halt the spread of Communism, and to contribute to the causes which, all around them, they can feel subverting the character of the American society they used to know. They are taught to love their neighbor and to treat every man as equal; and they are expected to pay to the blacks and others the debts which the established, having for generations gained their profits from slavery and the slums, are wealthy enough to avoid paying in person.

By and large, the lower-middle class is extremely patriotic; almost all have memories of worse days, less money in the pocket, no television in the home, no barbecue pit, no shiny and speedy car. America has been good to them. On the other hand, the price they pay for beer and television is a larger helplessness. Pragmatic, wealthy, educated men decide: questions of peace and war; the cost of living, inflation, deinflation; the placement of highways, schools, apartment houses, hospitals, airports; who will run for office and what his freedom of action will be; the direction of technological innovation; job opportunities—in a word, virtually every matter of life, well-being, and death. The lower-middle class lives in crowded houses. The work they are given to do has little relation to their own sensibilities, imagination, or creativity. They have not had psychiatric or other care to prepare them for the tensions that explode in their homes—the dissatisfactions of the women, the hostilities of the men, the resentments of the young.

Somewhere, far away in "Washington," some leaders are daily arranging, without consulting them, new ways to intensify the difficulties they face. And almost everywhere there seem to be "troublemakers" insulting everything they have at high expense held dear, and tearing down the structures in which they have so patiently and painstakingly been trying to gain at last a safe foothold.

John McDermott has written in *The Nation* of the resistance the young college students of the lower-middle class put up against the efforts of liberal professors to search out and to destroy their local, uneducated standards, aspirations, prejudices, and tastes. Operating from within a more national or international cultural framework, professors are by and large insensitive or hostile to the home culture of their students. On television and in the national press, students and parents can feel the same relentless pressure: enter into the national, technological, rationalized culture.

To be sure, "higher" standards of justice, due process, respect for fundamental rights and reform seem to have accompanied the extension of national power into local communities. More often than not, the federal government was on the side of little people against powerful local interests. But the model on which national power was extended has appeared increasingly to be abstract, heartless, and subservient to technological, bureaucratic imperatives. It is not only the traditionally conservative who, now more ritually than really, oppose "liberal bureaucracy." (Many conservatives have become fabulously wealthy in a welfare state aimed directly at the economic benefit of the upper-middle and middle classes: highways, airports, and new technological industries do not make the lower-middle class rich.) The lower-middle class has lost the sense of participation in shaping its own destiny.

How can the injustices done the lower-middle class by our society be remedied? The politician and the political party that can best answer that question will carry the large swing vote that will determine the direction of American policies in the 1970's. One key is furnished by an insight of the radical left, namely, that the most important class factor in the United States is knowledge; the elites of the present and future are knowledge elites. The lower-middle class requires credible means to check and to balance the power of experts. They will attain those means either by anti-intellectualism, anger, and reaction or by new, legitimized power.

The secondary but most easily articulated problems of the lower-middle class in a shifting society are how to shield home, income, and opportunity for advancement from the contingencies of a tumultuous time. The primary problem is how to regain a sense of purpose, honor, and dignity. An American needs to feel free; he has to feel equal to the next man—equal in opportunity and equal in attention paid his grievances. Unconsciously, the shift of the cultural center of gravity to national media of expression, and especially television, has led too many in our society to talk down to the little man, by undercutting his local standard of values and making him feel lost and out of his element. *He* doesn't talk the way television announcers, newsmen, analysts talk; he never went to school and doesn't understand the brief comments of experts. He is always left with the feeling that the big men in society are speaking to him in code. He judges by his local experience, and often that experience has not led him to encounter the sorts of problems that public spokesmen talk about; or else, if he has had comparable experiences, his own common sense leads him to different, even opposite, solutions from those publicly proposed. "I just can't understand why they let these long-haired kids (or North Koreans) get away with so much," he is likely to say; "I'd give 'em one good kick in the ass and that would be that!"

For the last twenty years, the direction of United States policies, international and domestic, have disproportionately benefitted the new class of technical experts and the already wealthy. The invisible poor of whom Michael Harrington wrote have been almost totally neglected; the lower-middle class, too. *The chief reason for this neglect is the influence of the anti-Communist military and intelligence establishment upon the priorities of scientific and technological progress.* Seventy percent of the U.S. budget goes to pay for present and past wars. The quality, decency, and stability of the life of the lower-middle class and the poor deteriorate annually under these priorities. The military budget could, and must be, cut at least in half. (It was eight billion dollars when Truman left office.) New priorities for federal moneys should be for assistance like tax rebates, cheaper federal loans, higher salaries, and other subsidies to people whose talent and abilities do not qualify them for higher education. No one should be penalized because his talents are not those of a technocrat.

Industries, like political control of communities, should be decentralized; rebates of federal taxes back to localities should cover higher costs. An investment in democratic participation is more important to our survival than investment in guns. Labor unions should acquire a voice in managerial decisions; workers should have a say in the production schedules, marketing, and advertising of their company's products, just as they should share profits and losses. Professor Jaroslav Vanek of Cornell has been working for several years on new concepts of worker creativity and responsibility, in keeping with individual initiative and corporate solidarity.

Participation in decision making on the job, in schools, and in government is the only possible way to fulfill the deepest demands of the American psyche. When Americans feel helpless, they know their democracy is sick. And nothing cures democracy quicker than people exercising real responsibility. The political party that invents ways of giving real political and economic power to the lower-middle class and to the poor, at the expense of the wealthy and the educated middle class, will have gone a long way towards making our future hopeful. At present we are descending deeper into the control of the many by the few, under the classical guise of needing to protect ourselves against outside aggressors.

7. A Nation with the Soul of a Church

"AMERICA," G. K. Chesterton once said, "is a nation with the soul of a church." He noted one characteristic in particular that makes America peculiar: "America is the only nation in the world that is founded on a creed."

Chesterton was right. The United States has become the birthplace of a major new religion. It is the religion of "the American way of life." The depths of American politics cannot be understood unless one understands that the United States is not just a nation but a way of life; and not just any old way of life, but a sacred and religiously honored one.

The new American religion is not Jewish, neither is it Christian. It is a new, and very limited, religion. If that religion does not soon change, its narrowness will destroy America and the world with it.

On American coins it says: "In God we trust." (On the belts of German SS troopers, it said: "*Gott mit Uns*"—"God with us.") In major presidential speeches, at major turning points in America's decisions, something would be symbolically and painfully lacking if the President of the United States did not invoke the name of God, speak of America's destiny "under God," and enunciate the sacred American mission to extend liberty and equality at home and abroad.

Americans who are pragmatic and realistic tend to underestimate the power of the religious symbols of the American way of life. Practical politicians do not. The most hard-boiled politicians find it necessary to speak often of God. And they commonly, as well, link God to America's manifest destiny, her purpose, her mission, her crusade in Europe, her desire for "peace with honor" in Vietnam. Politicians resolve to effect world peace and understanding on terms ordinary Americans can understand; that is to say, in American terms.

The American way of life is a missionary religion. American businessmen, intelligence agents, Green Berets, and ordinary soldiers willingly carry the American message to every continent. They operate from more than three thousand overseas military installations. (No other nation has as many as two hundred military installations on foreign soil.)

The American way of life is—as it says on the dollar bill—imagined to be a *"novus ordo seclorum,"* a new order of the ages, a new world, a new paradise, a new Eden, a new starting place in human history. It is imagined to be free from the entanglements, corruption, evils, sins, irrationalities, and machinations which have marked every other civilization in history. America was born as a land without a past, a virgin land, born on a fresh continent under a fresh constitution.

Thus the American religion regards Americans as being peculiarly innocent, peculiarly good, peculiarly untouched by the corruptions of history. Americans find it difficult to believe evil of themselves. Even when faced with the facts, they cannot allow themselves to believe that a Secretary of Defense can tell a Senate committee, behind closed doors, a brazen lie, as a recent Secretary did about the nature, mission, and activities of a US spy ship in the Gulf of Tonkin. It took four years to uncover that lie.

Americans scarcely believe that American boys can massacre women and children. They cannot imagine themselves approving of strategic, massive massacres through bombing raids, artillery barrages, and "search and destroy" operations that have already, by Defense Department figures, killed at least one million Vietnamese.

America is religiously imagined to be the home of the free and the brave, the land of liberty. Given the faith that they are born free, it is difficult for Americans to believe that they have surrendered their freedom to generals, heads of corporations, a handful of foreign policy advisors, and the operatives of the Central Intelligence Agency. Such circles, far more than Congress, determine the foreign policy and the economic priorities of the United States.

The American people do not criticize, or cut, or ridicule the vastest military budgets of any nation in human history, or control the treaties, pacts, agreements, resolutions for instant war-making, and various overseas activities which bind America to military intervention with scores of troubled nations. They do not protest the fact that recently generals testified to the Senate about plans for a war with China that would require, conservatively, three million American boys on Chinese soil in the first two years.

Americans like to imagine themselves as "leaders of the Free World." They speak the words "Free World" as they would voice a fundamentalist doctrine, not as an accurate description of real nations. Americans are not troubled by the large number of dictatorships and ruthlessly unjust regimes included as "free nations" among those happily supported by American taxes and troops.

The "silent majority" of whom Vice President Agnew and President Nixon so warmly speak are the major supporters of the new world religion of the American way of life. But there are many others in the "silent majority" who no longer quite believe in "that old-time religion" of the American way of life. There are true believers and there are people who have begun to notice new, strange changes in American religion.

For one thing, the old-fashioned American religion could not admit that America might ever suffer a defeat. "I will not be the first President to preside while the United States lost a war," President Johnson said, and President Nixon has echoed him. But what, in general religious terms, is wrong with losing a war, or being defeated, or being humiliated, or admitting that you were wrong? It goes against the American religion, but it certainly does not go against Christianity, for example, or against Judaism.

The American religion has three major motifs, which Presidents and other politicians may appeal to to their hearts' content. The first is the motif of new birth, of innocence, of a young idealistic nation. (The present generation is a threat to this motif precisely because it is the first to deny that the American flag is a symbol of idealism and innocence.)

The second motif is that of "malice towards none," of reconciliation in the midst of domestic quarrels, such as that which followed the Civil War. The Civil War was until that time the most bitter and violent war in history. But President Lincoln created a new motif which made reconciliation possible.

The third motif is the "manifest destiny" of the United States to expand its interests and to find ever new frontiers: not only in the Pacific, and in Latin America, but also in every corner of the planet and in outer space as well. We are God's people. ("God is our co-pilot.") We intervene everywhere for him.

The American religion has as yet no motif that recognizes the limitations, arrogance, mistakes, and sins of America as a nation. Possibly a third of the American people are ready to voice such accusations about the American presence in the rest of the world. Possibly another third are bitterly opposed to this direct criticism of their own self-congratulatory religious views. ("America: Love it or leave it.") But it is likely that another third would be swayed by the example of the closest thing the American religion has to a high priest: the President of the United States.

If the President of the United States could admit that in some certain respect the policies of the United States were mistaken, incorrect, and even immoral, and that we must repent and change them, many Americans would agree. For they are not so fundamentalist that they expect lightning to strike any man who says that America is not entirely godly. The American religion is capable of adding the motif that America has sinned, even grievously, and is capable of growing in stature thereby.

8. Politics as Witness

Two things about Eugene McCarthy become clear in his book, *The Year of the People*.[1] The first is that an ancient construction on politics has been reintroduced into American consciousness, namely, that politics occurs in the zone of *maya,* or illusion, a zone in which there is no truth and no falsehood, no pure evil and no savior. The role of the serious politician, then, is ultimately to be a witness, and by no means is he either to pretend to bring salvation or to rest the whole weight of his effort on practical attainments.

"The year of the people" was the year the people "bore witness." They did not end the war in Vietnam, or solve the problems of American cities. Yet they lived up to the best that was in them. Their *being* shone through, and *being* weighs heavier on the final scale than *doing.* For in this vale of tears, human doing is never successful; we work in the harsh light of eternity, in which our being is scrutinized.

Being is never separable from doing, however. *Agere sequitur esse.* Acting follows from being. If McCarthy had not announced his long, hard march in November 1967, his being would have been suspect. His actions revealed who he was. But who he was was even more important in his eyes than any number of actions for action's sake.

A Protestant America, a pragmatic America, would never understand the springs of the man, philosophical or emotional. For to be American in spirit is to value doing more than being. Journalists and supporters always wanted McCarthy to *do* more. The myth their emotions run by fears silence and hiatus; their

[1] New York, 1969.

70

secret musical score calls for constant *crescendo* or at least *andante*.

But McCarthy's myth was different; the drums he listened to went differently. They were drums of being, which imagined that not all the dancing and music of all the world's witch doctors would cure America's ills. What just might help America a little ("in politics," wrote Aristotle, "we must be satisfied with a tincture of excellence") was a new pedagogy, a new myth, a myth that placed being, reality, truth ahead of acting, hoping, future.

Eugene McCarthy wanted to be himself in 1968 and to let the people find in him a mirror of themselves. "The man the people found" wanted to teach the people that they already had in themselves the resources of a new politics: drop the frenetic doing, the shouting, the midnight meetings, and respect the limitations and harsh beauties of their own reality. An America able to *be* itself, without doing so much, might prevent itself from destroying the world.

Being before doing: it is an ancient Catholic theme. McCarthy retains in himself something priestly. He made it his primary purpose to regard, and to teach others to regard, politics as a vocation. And what is a vocation? A call. A call, above all else, not to be successful but to be witness. To what? To all those values that make human life more than beastly: to honesty, courage, community, freedom; to peace, justice, truth, brotherliness. And in any case, *against* brazen lies, wanton destructiveness, absurd priorities.

A vocation is a call from elsewhere. Even if no one in the world responds to one's witness, still, one acts *sub specie aeternitatis*. And in that burning light many temporal efforts seem little more than ludicrous. The politician works in the same zone as the poet, but he does not often enough lift his eyes from the dancing shadows.

Because McCarthy did not take history, politics, and time with ultimate seriousness, he was accused of laziness, untrustworthiness, betrayal, and of having a "*Commonweal* Catholic" willingness to end up second-rate. (Whereas everybody knows that "Kennedy Catholics" are satisfied with nothing less than finishing first.) But if one looks critically at the record of American activists—those whom Norman Mailer dubs "christians"—is it, in human terms, worthy of emulation? The American myth is the myth of the agent, the doer, the initiator, the intervener. The aim is to make history over, or even "to get America moving again."

The McCarthy spirit is in fundamental contradiction to this. For that reason alone, he affected us all deeply, and we remain unsatisfied by analyses of him that end up with disappointment and appeal to some "enigma." The enigma is in ourselves. McCarthy revealed something about ourselves, about America, about human life that we resist, that we cannot get conscious enough about to put into words. And we are restless. It was not entirely *his* fault. It is not quite true that *he* let *us* down.

The second thing *The Year of the People* confirms is the poetic, highly moral, self-directed character of the man himself. Quite apart from his philosophy, Senator McCarthy's own personality intensifies the distance between him and other major politicians. During the campaign, he once prayed at a private mass that he might never tell an untruth in the campaign. "I think we did pretty well by that," he nodded, rubbing his nose, when I recalled the incident to him.

I do not know McCarthy's character at all, except publicly. I retain two impressions from the one two-hour meeting I had with him. First, he thinks ahead for those who may be following him; he feels a relationship of obligation to his constituency. Whatever he did after the convention was done with the thought of gradually displacing the affections of millions—possibly so that there will not be, in his case, a cult of personality, and possibly also so that he himself will have maximum freedom of action for paths that may be unpopular and lonely. Secondly, I retain the impression of a man storing his spiritual energy for possibly the most difficult thing he has had to do. A poet perhaps, reflecting, meditating, taking his time.

The year 1968 may have been "the year of the people." In some peculiar way, it was not the year for Eugene McCarthy. He was not entrapped by it, and he entrapped no one. He did what was in him, when no one else would act. An ambitious man, he knows he would make a superior President. He wanted very badly to be President—much more than the press could ever perceive. But he wanted the Presidency on his own terms, his kind of Presidency: to reveal being, both his own and that of the nation. (It is not by accident that he speaks of himself as "we," a little like a pope, vicar of a people.) He would not falsify himself or the nation in his search for the Presidency. He would pursue his own course, and if it were God's will, nothing would be lacking in his own effort; he would not lose through any fault of his own. But he would not falsify.

Eugene McCarthy is a strangely free man. The adjectives used of him—"aloof," "cold," "proud"—all begins to make sense if one feels a little afraid of a free man. For a free man runs by his own laws. Those who learn about human beings, or politicians, by studying what happens among the general run of men are bound to find themselves out of their depth when they find a man whose law is his own.

The question the McCarthy candidacy leads us to ask is: Can a free man ever become President of the United States? (Are Hubert Humphrey or Richard Nixon our ideals of free men?)

Some may recall that many of the adjectives noted above were also used of John F. Kennedy. Both were distinctively Catholic men, deeply embedded in the sensibility and imagination of the Catholic people—the one in an easier-going Midwest, and experienced in the Benedictine seminary; the other in harsh, aggressive Boston, and not well-educated in the tradition, not at all monastic.

Both knew the final end and absurdity of history. Both have made an irrevocable witness. Both cherished the pain and lonely ways of liberty. Kennedy played with fire in cooperating with the establishment in the Democratic Party, the cities, the Pentagon, and in the intelligence agencies. But McCarthy was determined to cut a more independent path.

The American system was not ready for either man; it prefers artificial hearts.

Because Robert Kennedy could get to Mayor Daley and to

the white, lower-middle class—to the Wallace vote and "the silent majority," as well as to the blacks—I finally took my chances in 1968 with him. I did so with no loss of respect for the unparalleled and indispensable contribution of Eugene McCarthy to American history. Politics is a vocation. And, in the end, witness is everything. What *The New York Review of Books* has called "The Ultra-Resistance" is, indeed, basically Catholic. In the darkness that may be ahead of us, a politics of witness may be the only one left us. Whether for the weak or for the powerful, it is the least destructive politics.

Education
for the Counter-Culture

9. Americanizing, Simonizing

PART of the subtitle of Helmut Thielicke's *Nihilism*—"a Christian Answer"—may be misleading.[1] A Christian should *pursue* the experience of nothingness. He does not have an "answer" to it. He must, like everyone else, interpret it. For hardly anyone can become a sensitive, intelligent adult in the modern world without experiencing those feelings of strangeness, emptiness, and dread to which the words "nihilism" and "nothingness" point. Some men have made out of these feelings an argument for concentration camps, sadism, and moral heedlessness. Others have made out of them an argument for man's total responsibility for himself and for others. Some men have heard in them the silence of the true God; others the silence of an unattended universe. In one way or another these experiences must be interpreted. Even to ignore them, to flee from them, to repress them, is to foist an interpretation on them: that they are unreal, unimportant, misleading, frightening.

Why is it that the modern world has become the chosen arena of such feelings? (The word "nihilism" was first used at the beginning of the nineteenth century; later its use became widespread through the stories of Turgenev and Dostoevsky and through the unsparing analyses of Nietzsche.) Professor Thielicke deals with the experience of nothingness in Europe after World War II, and traces the development of the "ism" which attempts to interpret that experience.

But what about America? For a long time optimistic, busy mastering a continent and then the world and outer space, emphasizing upbeat, the American psyche seemed impervious to the experience of nothingness. Norman Vincent Peale ex-

1 New York, 1961.

pressed a characteristic theme in the business ethic of American life, under which President Nixon (as under President Eisenhower) found symbolic amplification through the White House: the power of positive thinking.[2] Businessmen and engineers, although university trained, have long retained in their ranks a relatively high proportion of believers in God; a majority of scientists, artists, professors—intellectuals—in the United States do not believe in God.[3] Yet even among the intellectuals, many in the United States have disclaimed awareness of the anxiety, dread, and estrangement that European writers make central in their thinking. Philosophers like Charles Frankel (*The Love of Anxiety*) and Sidney Hook (*The Quest For Being*), and social thinkers like Daniel Bell (*The End of Ideology*) have embraced an optimistic, comfortable pragmatism that embodies a metaphysics of gradual progress, democratic soundness, and middle-class contentment. It is likely that most American natural scientists and social scientists, in their attachment to rational and functional wholes and their aversion to past traditions of pessimism and historical, non-rational complexity, maintain a comfortable optimism about human progress. Progress is their most important value.

From the point of view of the experience of nothingness, however, claims to human progress are as illusory as any others. History may be going nowhere in particular. The individual human being, as well as the entire social organism, meet today exactly the same fate as formerly: alienation, estrangement, death. Democratic forms of life do not prevent a nation from becoming militarist, counter-revolutionary, and racist. Technological advancement is morally neutral. Technical mastery over his environment makes man rather than nature his own foremost enemy. Is *that* prospect benevolent? Scientific method as presently conceived is put to use through the myth that knowledge is power; and the power created by that method may be used to predict, to control, and to annihilate human behavior, rather than to enlighten it. Moreover, the myth of knowledge

2 See "Norman Vincent Peale Is Criticized, but Many Listen to His Message," *The Wall Street Journal* (May 7, 1969).
3 Seymour Lipset, "American Intellectuals: Their Politics and Status," *Political Man* (New York, 1963), pp. 332–371.

as power makes the self-knower a manipulator of his own psyche: divides him into two, master and material, therapist and patient. Was the ancient division of man into body and spirit more destructive of human integrity than the modern division into observer and observed? Is the image of man as a consciousness modulating the flow of his own pleasures and pains sophisticated or decadent?

The experience of nothingness defined: that experience in which a man perceives that his former perceptions were structured in a way they did not have to be, in an arbitrary and unnecessary way. *There is no one obligatory way to perceive things.* A kind of giddiness and dizziness arise. One's former goals, aims, purposes now seem suspended in air. The structure one had put into existence one pulls out. The unity of one's life slips from one's grasp, dissolves. Raw, tumultuous experience is overwhelming: How can one shape it, manage it, reduce it to form? Action is problematical because no goal at all seems more valuable, more useful, or more attractive than any other. It is as though at the heart of the human animal there were a love of dissolution, a longing to split into a million measureless particles and fly apart in scattered mist. The experience of nothingness is an experience of the formlessness at the heart of human consciousness. We exist only through form; the experience of our formlessness is terrifying. We know our kinship to nothingness. We dread being reminded of it.

A middle-class life is stable because its forms have the power of myth. Those forms silently shape perceptions and expectations. Hunger, disease, ignorance, confusion, violence and risk —for most of the human beings in human history the stuff of existence—are kept outside the hedges of the suburbs. It is no wonder that young people of the middle class can hardly understand the philosophy and literature of the humanities; they have had little experience of what most historical peoples meant by "humanity." What is remarkable is that the new radical young have in the last few years seen through the illusions of scientific, technical, democratic stability. They have tasted nothingness. Their refusal to accept the most powerful fantasy of security ever attained by human beings is one of the great spiritual triumphs of history. Their lack of spiritual discipline, of a tradition of dealing with nothingness, makes their triumph fragile and dangerous.

A middle-class life promises the safe attainment of individuality. The truth is that growth in knowledge of oneself is growth in knowledge of one's ignorance. Growth in command over oneself is growth in impulsiveness, fantasy, free association, and direct response. Growth in fidelity to oneself is (in one key respect) growth in a sense of isolation from one's environment and from others. The more of an individual one becomes, the less tractable, affable, docile, group-centered, and other-centered one becomes. Life in a capitalist technical society (or indeed in a socialist technical society) is a contradiction between the demands of teamwork and the demands of the impulsive self. "If everyone does what he pleases," the capitalist worries, "imagine the resulting chaos." "Not chaos," the anarchist smiles. "Rugged individualism."

Moreover, even the artist—the paragon of an integrated spirit—finds his own life sheering off in unrelated directions. The more he comes to know his own creations, the more refracted, mirror-like, and fathomless his own consciousness seems to be. The novelist's characters, however full of life, are totally at the beck and call of his eraser and restless pen. And which of the narrator's several voices are the artist's true voice? The artist himself is often the worst judge of that, as great artists slyly suspect. Who knows, then? The more one explores the resources of one's consciousness—beyond the accepted social roles and cultural myths—the more ignorant one comes to seem. We are strangers to ourselves. Alienation does not arise because our creativity is not reflected in our labor, as Marx avers. Or, at least, besides *that* alienation there is another, far more profound, which arises from the inner formlessness which yields to the most arduous explorer's mocking laughter.

The professor, however. There's a man who should know his way around the edges of the nothingness. Well-paid, intelligent, certified by his scientific peers, in charge, an expert: a priestly type if ever a society had one. "Professor, exorcise my nothingness." "My son, be more objective. Regard not feelings. Disci-

80

pline thyself to measurement. Be clear. Formulate a testable proposition. What does it mean to feel 'nothingness'? Ah, a specific feeling, isn't it? So it isn't 'nothingness,' then, literally, is it? Now what was it you had for breakfast? When was the last time you had a good fu—, that is, had, well, relations?" "Bacon and eggs, professor. All last night. And yourself?" The professor speaks as the mouthpiece of an eminent profession, not as a person; he deftly turns aside the reference to himself and proceeds to speak objectively. "But, professor, that's my trouble. I hear you speaking, but in some other world. Where is that objective world? Your clarity rests upon—? . . . A precise use of language. And language, professor, it lends itself to precise use? . . . Ah, if I acquire the proper discipline . . . And if I refuse?"

Everything is arbitrary. Like medieval scholastics, philosophers may argue that clarity of thought is therapeutic, or even that there is, somewhere, a logic that constitutes a universal framework of reasonable discourse. But always, one notices, such men insist upon an apprenticeship for neophytes; they demand an asceticism, a disciplining of one's feelings, impulses, habits, perceptions. "And why that particular discipline? . . . Ah, I see. So that I may perceive *objectively*. So that I may be numbered among *the reasonable*."

The experience of nothingness arises when one perceives the questionableness of every form whatsoever. Even facts may be questioned, since they may have been incorrectly perceived, ordered, or transmitted. Nothing is perceived except from a point of view. And from whose point of view are correct points of view to be selected? The root of the experience of nothingness is man's capacity to question everything whatsoever, including his own capacity to question. Man is in some way all things, as Aristotle said, because his capacity for wonder (questioning) is absolutely unlimited and hence he may adapt himself to the contours of anything. Man is in some way all things; and therefore kin to nothingness.

But if the experience of nothingness is rooted in the human capacity for questioning, and arises when that capacity is exercised and grows strong, then that experience is not a sign of illness but of health, not of decline but of growth, not of aberration but of maturity. Moreover, the experience of nothingness has already built into it, as it were, the seeds of its own further development. Unless a man has the courage and the honesty to raise the relevant questions, the experience of nothingness does not arise for him. Many don't have it. Many live contentedly in the forms they have inherited from others. The experience of nothingness comes as a *breakthrough,* for which honesty and courage provide the requisite force. It comes with its own certification of authority. Authenticity is a twofold awareness: that one has acted with honesty and courage, and that total honesty and courage are never available to us. (The authentic man does not imagine himself to *be* honest and courageous.) The experience of nothingness is not imaginable apart from honesty and courage, even when it arises by accident, unasked for, uninvited.

The usual description of the experience of nothingness has European lineage. Nietzsche analyzed the experience from many different perspectives in the first part of *The Will to Power.* Kafka's novels, *The Trial* and *The Castle,* and his story *Metamorphosis* allow us to enter into a feeling of loss, horror, and dreadful helplessness. Sartre's *No Exit* and *Nausea* explore the alienation of the Cartesian consciousness ("I think, therefore *I* am"—as if *I* were merely an isolated consciousness) from its own body, from its physical environment, and from other people. Albert Camus saw his work as an effort to begin within the experience of nothingness—to accept it as a given in modern civilization—and to construct out of it an "ethic of happiness." The hero of *The Stranger* achieves joy by making a decision to keep both his imminent execution and his longing for love and understanding fused. The irreconcilable tension between the *nostalgia* for harmony and the *absurdity* of concrete life gives birth to the sense of the *absurd:* a triumph of honesty and courage, a willingness to endure (and even to scorn) the "polar night" and the futility. Tutored by the immense malice of Hitler's version of nihilism, Camus struggles to find a social ground on which men who cannot deny the experience of nothingness can, nevertheless, united in their suffering and mutual vulnerability, struggle to diminish the number of those who suffer.

The usual history of the experience of nothingness points out how the forms, structures, and symbols which had made men in the West feel comfortable with one another, like partners who each had a role and station in an historic, cosmic destiny, suffered one shock after another. Culture is constituted by consciousness, given shape by a way of perceiving and understanding and acting. Western consciousness rested for a long time upon three fundamental images: that each man is equally precious in God's sight; that God holds each accountable for his historical actions, which coalesce in the general building up of a new historical order ("Thy kingdom come, on earth as it is in heaven"); and that all phenomena of human experience, no matter how random or trivial, are comprehended and united in the mind of God. Thus men could feel that everything they might experience was related, had a place, offered at least a hidden, ultimate meaning—nothing wasted, nothing random, nothing unconnected. When belief in God faltered, belief in science took its place—belief in that underlying Logos to which even Freud expressed loyalty in *The Future of an Illusion,* a central intelligibility to be ever more thoroughly penetrated through the cultivation of science.

The experience of nothingness arose when men glimpsed the possibility that human life may not be structured either by a personal God or by an impersonal reason—that neither religion nor science give adequate shape to man's experiences and his questions. The forms inherited from religion and scientific progress are comforting, many agreed. But what if they do not apply? Dostoevsky's "underground man" thought thoughts that neither religion nor science sanctioned, felt dizziness and vertigo springing up from a fundamental formlessness: *nothing* shapes our experience adequately, every form is but a mythical projection. *Reason itself* is not a foundation but an instrument; not a guarantor of progress but a fertile source of illusion and false security. Science does not tell us what *the world* is like; it gives back to us mirror images of our own symbols, answering only those questions we happen to frame. The cult of reason led to the establishment of insane asylums, the attempt to banish the irrational from society—an attempt that was itself mad. Ironically, the metaphors for modern "rational" society that have come to dominate modern social consciousness are those of a mad house, a hospital, a prison, a labyrinth, a darkling plain.

Surely, it may now be most useful for an American audience to address the question: Why does the younger generation of the most affluent and most "highly developed" nation of the world feel keenly the attractions of nihilism? What is the physiognomy of the experience of nothingness as it occurs, ever more frequently, in the United States?

The image that has controlled the development of American culture is that of "the melting pot." That image was always misleading, for in fact a Nordic, Anglo-Saxon consciousness dominated American life, a Protestant consciousness, setting the style for what might be experienced, intuited, and decided. In order to prosper in the United States, possibly even to survive in the United States, immigrants from other ways of life had to pay a price. That price was the Americanization of their psyches. They had to cease being what they were, and to learn the ways of Nordic, Anglo-Saxon culture in its setting in the new world.

The dominant political and intellectual metaphor shaping American consciousness is that of the marketplace. Human beings are to think of themselves as atomic particles flowing into and out of a free marketplace. (The cocktail party replaces the communal eucharist as the ritual model of the movement of individuals in a group.) Individuals have value if they are productive citizens; that is, if they bring contributions to the marketplace and promote the mechanisms of the marketplace. Free speech and civil rights are mechanisms through which the underlying vision is made to serve intellectual inquiry and political self-governance. Society is an impersonal mechanism, promoting in individuals their consciousness of themselves as rational, productive individuals. Each is in ultimate isolation from others, although cooperating with others and cherishing teamwork as indispensable to the working of the system. It requires functional analysis to describe the workings of a mechanism: the myth of a machine is the underlying shaper of consciousness.

Why is the metaphor of a mechanism so dear to Nordic, Anglo-Saxon culture in the United States? Here one's reflections are forced to a level where uncertainty cannot be eliminated. It is clear that there is a *coincidence* between the shape that social and cultural consciousness takes in the United States (and in other Nordic, Anglo-Saxon lands) and the requirements of a technical, capitalistic civilization. Which came first? Did a certain style of consciousness give rise to a technical, capitalistic economic order? Or did the incipient economic order gradually give shape to the style of consciousness required for its survival and uninhibited growth? If men think of themselves primarily as individuals, organized functionally through an impersonal system, they will presumably be able to accept a differentiation of roles, specialization, teamwork, competition, the rationalization of inputs and outputs, efficiency, and the other triumphs of analytic reason over the rest of the psyche required for a technical, capitalistic civilization. Moreover, their view of themselves will be self-verifying. They count the achievement of isolated individuality—lack of constraint by others, independence, *laissez faire,* self-sufficienty—as the criterion of freedom and thus the zenith in human achievement; but the workings of a highly rationalized capitalistic system are guaranteed to heighten their isolation from one another. They will live alone in their own heads. As Leibniz wrote, monads have no windows. The myth of the rugged individual will not be weakened by the demands of cooperation, teamwork, efficiency, and rationalization; for the companion myth of functional mechanism does not demand the penetration of one impermeable particle by another, but only a certain sensitivity to signals from others such that frictions and collisions are minimized. David Riseman properly described Americans as a lonely crowd. Even in their own families they are lonely. The Beatles sing: "She's leaving home/After living alone so many years."

Understandably, the cultivation of characteristics like affability, personableness, hale good fellowship, frequent smiles, a

85

friendly manner become the chief preoccupation of families, schools, and industry itself. For since a crowd is not a community, and since the social system is a mechanism, people must be taught to make personal gestures as if it were a community. The terror of being a pawn in so huge an impersonal mechanism would be intolerable unless receptionists, airline hostesses, television announcers, and others in roles where "human relations" are salient reassured us with signs of human feeling that are genuine if possible, mimetic if necessary. (The hostess does not have to *feel* like smiling, or even to *like* the one to whom her smile is directed; her job is to smile anyway.) The possession of "personality," as if it were a commodity, is an economic asset of great value to many lucky individuals; their services are required to help make the American system seem human.

Americanization demands a great price of persons from cultures where other fundamental myths hold sway. In some cultures, the capacity for analytic reason is not so highly developed; one is not shaped to think of oneself as an isolated self but as a brother inseparable from a community; connectedness with one's impulses, feelings, fantasies, and idiosyncracies is valued more highly than promptitude, regularity, a precise sense of time and function, a willingness to separate one's moods from one's work, a love for efficiency and other values required for a productive life in the American model. Thus, acculturated Americans frequently find Indians, Negroes, Southern Europeans, South Vietnamese, Latin Americans, and others irresponsible, shiftless, lazy, selfish, unreliable, moody, oversexed, enigmatic, rhythmic, earthy, intuitive, loose, cool, and so forth. It takes a lot of discipline and training to make the raw material of most of humanity "shape up" and become productive in the American mold.

Americans wear wrist watches which divide their actions into efficient, regular, and rational segments. They discipline their eating habits both by cutting down the time allotted and making the foods as bland (hamburgers, cokes, sandwiches) and as standardized as possible. They train themselves to be "objective" in conversations and to listen carefully to one another's words, blocking out as much as possible of the feeling tone flowing back and forth between speakers. The capacities their schools seem to be chiefly concerned with developing are two: the capacities to store information and to analyze it. The fact that adolescents and young adults are at the height of their sexual powers, bursting with impulses, fantasies, and carefully repressed emotions, associations, and compulsions hardly enters into the purview of the schools. The daily rubbing out of pre-historic memory traces, of sensitive and subtle perceptions of character and action such as is manifested by unschooled peoples the world over, and of an external richness and orneriness that characterized American life even two generations ago—such losses for the human spirit are scarcely mourned.

In a word, the fundamental American myth—deeper even than the myth of the lonely individual and the myth of the marketplace, because presupposed by both of them—is the myth of the head, of the mind, of the importance of words, rationality, and impersonal logic. The ordinary white American seems to imagine himself as a consciousness encased in a bag of skin. He looks at his body, it appears, as something he possesses, a foreign casing, of which he is somewhat uncertain and ashamed. He holds his hand in front of him and thinks of it as an object out there. One of his most serious problems, both philosophically and emotionally, is the mind-body problem: How can he communicate from in here out through his body and over to someone else's body and emotions, and thence to his "objective" mind? The problem of communication is imagined as a gap: self separated from self, flashing semaphore signals through bodily motions. The most highly developed human capacities (of all the possible human capacities) among white Americans appear to be the capacity for storing information and the capacity for analyzing it: those capacities most imitable by machines. It is as if the higher race of the future, which men should even now emulate, is a race of machines created by man to supersede himself. It is as if in writing their own history that future race will point out its forerunners among humans: those who were most logical, analytical, machinelike, and especially the Nordic, Anglo-Saxon Americans.

To live up to the myth of the head, and to be worthy of such a future, the human being of other cultural streams must undertake a grueling discipline. He must cease imagining himself as part of the earth, a fruit of the earth in the same way that blossoms, apples, chipmunks, and lions are fruits of earth. He must cease imagining himself at one with earth, alert to its rhythms, its sad cycles of life and vitality and struggle and death. He must uproot himself, become rational. Beats and rhythms of the waters, of the lands, must cease running through his blood. His blood must be quieted. Every natural outpouring of his body—hair, odor, breath—must be submitted to machine processes, eradicated, kept at bay. (All evening on television, ritual war on the human body is acted out: scrub, rinse, deodorize, sanitize. The body is evil. Rational processes rationally arrived at must supplant every instinctual, libidinous, bloody, vital trace. The Manichens triumph—and even nudity, sexual orgy, and sensual delight come on glossy pages, glossy screens, mass-produced, shrewdly observed and analyzed.)

First, then, in order to be Americanized, a man must retreat into his head, his body always under the sway and pressure of mind, proudly stiff and decorous and controlled. He must be alienated from himself, divided into two, observer and observed. (A ceiling person always watches himself act; a door person simply acts. From floor to ceiling: step one.)

Secondly, in order to be Americanized, a man must be alienated from all organic, rhythmic, sensual, emotional, biological connectedness with the earth. Reason and efficiency should determine his activity; his biological urges, emotional preferences, fantasies, and impulses should be relegated to second place, inhibited, controlled, tread under. He should think of the earth as matter to be mastered; time is to be cut down, used efficiently, or killed. Value is measured by productivity, by contributions to society, by having, and by doing; not by being. Everything is a means; even ends are further means. The category of the future is uppermost. History replaces Nature; Nordic man replaces Mediterranean man (as Camus notes in *The Rebel*). Work replaces play as the measure of value.

Thirdly, in order to be Americanized, a man must be alienated from others. Others are separate from oneself. One does not perceive the ways in which others live in oneself, and oneself in them; one does not stress the primacy of the communal in human experience. Even though the sense of reality is a communal construction, and even though language is a social phenomenon, still, the American myth imagines that privacy and individuality are primary in our experience. Not only are others separate from oneself—walled up inside themselves, just as one's self experiences an inability to break out of one's own skin—but they are also competitors. At every step in one's development in America, one man's success is another's failure. In school, the slow child learns how to control himself lest, constantly humiliated by those who are first in the class, he run shrieking from the room at every mistake. Success, not achievement, becomes the category of mythic fulfillment. In some cultures, to congratulate a winning athlete is to evoke astonishment and confusion: he did the best that was in him as others did, and their mutual achievement, not invidious comparison of one with another, was the point of the effort. Struggle is the way to realize oneself, not to come out ahead of others. The example of others teaches one to outdo oneself, to measure one's own *being,* not to measure one's relative *position.*

Alienated from his own body, from his environment, and from others, the fully Americanized person—a caricature, an abstract picture, no doubt—shows a myth that cannot long be maintained. Under the pressures of scarcity, the depression, wars, and the struggle for familial security, recent generations of Americans could "forget themselves" and "sacrifice themselves for their children." That is, they could repress their instincts and give themselves to hard work, in order to obtain an advantageous position in the productive system. They chose this line of action so that their children "would have a chance to attend to the finer things in life." Their children now have that chance. The values and myths by which their parents lived are collapsing by their own weight. Many in the younger generation, seeing in the forms, structures, and symbols of the past quite different meaning than their parents saw, feel the form of consciousness of the civilization they inherit as a foreign object. Many do not yet see other forms with which to replace them.

In the ensuing formlessness, they taste the experience of nothingness. Without an image by which to shape themselves, how do they know how to make sense of their experience, or who they are? They do not want to mutilate their experience. But experience pours in upon them in overwhelming ways, like the riotous reverberations of their electronic music, like the spinning strobe lights whose revolutions are a second short of disorienting everyone.

Without a myth about their relationship to earth better than that of the master over matter; without a myth about their relationship to others better than that of the marketplace; without a myth about themselves better than that of the screen of consciousness therapeutically registering subtle measures of pleasure over pain—without a new culture—how can they escape the feeling that one value is as good as another, one action as useless as another, one ambition as meaningless as another? Creators must create. And it is the ageless challenge to creators that they must be able to create out of nothingness. No one can escape the conditions of human freedom. To remain in the experience of nothingness longer than two seconds is freely to have chosen it. For not to choose is also an exercise of freedom. The experience of nothingness is not an ending point. It is a starting point. What we are to do with it is a matter for shaping as we will. My own instincts run towards play, invention, connectedness with earth, community, honesty, courage—all those things without which the experience of nothingness could never have arisen. For we would not have such a fruitful and precious experience, arming us against the pretensions of structures and institutions howsoever vast, were it not for our brothers who went before us, teaching us how to question who we are and whence we came, teaching us to love the night as our true home.

Those who seek the night, desiring no security, are alone secure. The drive to question knows no resting place. How is it, then, that trusting it the people of the night know rest?

10. The Absolute Future

AMERICAN Catholics down the years have committed grievous sins of rabid anti-Communism. Consequently, one of the main imperatives of Catholics at present is to puncture the popular myths, biases, and prejudices about Communism that distort American political debate. On the international scene, the time has come for Christians and Marxists no longer merely to ignore or to destroy one another, but to learn from one another and to criticize one another. The shedding of one another's blood is useless, the ignoring of one another is empty.

One of the main points at which the current dialogue between Christians and Marxists converges is the meaning of the future. Contrary to stereotype, Marxist philosophy is not materialistic in a Western sense; it hopes for a future in which men's capacities of imagination, decision, and creative labor will be completely developed. Such a future may never, in fact, arrive; thus, the Marxist conception of the future might well be open. In that case, the function of the concept of future would be to provide leverage for criticism and reform of the present. *Secularia semper reformanda.*

At a conference of Catholics and Marxists in Austria, Karl Rahner defined Christianity in a perspective that might make sense to Marxists: "Christianity is the religion of the absolute future." Rahner's point is familiar to students of Reinhold Niebuhr. Christianity is eschatological; it refuses to call any present social arrangement final; within history, justice is never complete. Christianity refuses to idolize the present or the past, for its Lord is one who is ever to be awaited: "Come, Lord Jesus!" Christians are committed to building up the kingdom of God on earth, a kingdom of truth, liberty, justice, and love.

Since we do not yet have an international social order characterized by such values, Christians cannot very well rest upon what has so far been achieved; the pilgrimage is not over; there are many painful miles yet to march. *Ecclesia semper reformanda.*

Marxist thinkers have always had a predilection for one of the rather neglected Christian traditions, that of Joachim of Flora, the Anabaptists, and the Free Churches. The more established Christian traditions—Catholic, Lutheran, and Calvinist—have preferred to work in continuity with the institutions of the Holy Roman Empire. They have found it possible to work out various arrangements with emperors, kings, princes, and later with parliaments and economic corporations. They have operated on the assumption that there is a natural, created base for Christianity—a set of pre-Christian or religious or human values on which Christianity can "build." They have been more or less protective of the "moral fiber" of society, of its educational system and its family mores. They are proud of an entity they call "Western civilization," which they think of as "Christian."

By contrast, Joachim of Flora preached a coming "third age" of the Holy Spirit discontinuous with the pagan institutions, laws, and orders of the past. Anabaptists and Free Churchmen regarded the classical Lutheran and Calvinist reformations as "halfway reformations," much too limited in scope. For under Lutherans and Calvinists, as under Catholics, the establishment of religion remained intact; the social and economic institutions of the pagan past were still being "baptized." Free Churchmen desired a less institutionalized, more voluntary, more demanding church. Their desires were so exigent that the future became a crucial category in their thought. Some of them used the future as escape from the present; but still more of them used it as a weapon of criticism against the present. They demanded an authenticity, an integrity, and a commitment that empowered many poor and simple people to stand firm against feudal and monarchical institutions, and to generate much momentum for change in Western society.

In American theological thought, Harvey Cox stands more

nearly than any other in this tradition. It is not surprising, then, that Cox is the Christian theologian most sensitively attuned to the Christian-Marxist dialogue and the importance of the category of the future. In his rejoinder in *The Secular City Debate*,[1] in fact, he promised us an approach to language about God through language about the future. Such an enterprise will be at the heart of the issue between Marxists and Christians. Since the basic notion seems sound, I would like to help the project along by voicing a few critical reflections.

In the first place, Marxist thought regards existentialism as a stage in the progressive decadence of the West. In the Marxist view, existentialism has not healed the split between thought and action which is the disease of Western philosophy. Western philosophy is too "intellectualist"; it does not give sufficient weight to the fact that the role of thought is not merely to reflect the world, but to *change* the world. Again, it does not give sufficient weight to the fact that thinking is highly conditioned by social, economic, and other circumstances. Harvey Cox is not especially interested in epistemological questions, but he has been convinced by the Marxist critique that existentialism is a mere emotional retreat, a philosophy of inaction and Hamlet-like reflection, a disease of inwardness. Moreover, he has joined the Marxist critique of inwardness to Bonhoeffer's complaint about still another kind of inwardness: the concern and anxiety which German and Scandinavian religious thought has cherished as "the religious dimension" of man's subjective life.

Nevertheless, both for Marxist thought and for Cox, the source of thought which changes the world lies in the imagination, the projects, and the decisions of men. The future does not merely happen; men must invent it and take responsibility for it. For both, moreover, responsibility is not merely a factor of social conditioning; first one man must stand firm and then another—decision must well up from the strength of each individual. Otherwise, there is no maturity, only docility, passivity, and conformity.

[1] Edited by Daniel Callahan (New York, 1966).

Existentialist emphasis on decision making often seems to be too emotive and individualistic; even social relations are conceived on the model of eye-to-eye, deeply personal "encounters." With Marxist thinkers, Cox insists on the social dimensions and social realities of responsibility; much less than, say, Camus' Meursault in *The Stranger* will he allow a man to contemplate morosely his own emotional complexities. Does Cox at this point run the risk of evasion, promoting the reform of institutions because the reform of oneself is so difficult? There are some passages in *The Secular City*—particularly those on the "I-you relationship"—which read like the rationalizations of a busy, harried man. But to criticize Cox in this way would be to acquiesce in a dualism that is untenable. The individual and the social are not, in reality, separate; our language and hence even our private thoughts and our personal values are social phenomena. Cox is right to insist that maturity arises through social and political commitment. An accurate criticism, perhaps, is that he has not yet told us very much about how to choose among, or how to criticize, alternative commitments; he has merely announced where he stands.

But even at this point Cox's rejoinder in *The Secular City Debate* offers promise. "In our time the metaphysicians," he writes, "instead of integrating our lives for us, will probably more often challenge the premature integrations and cultural foreclosures that constrict us. . . . Our task today is to transmute the answers of classical metaphysics into questions that will guard the openness of our symbol worlds today." (I think Cox is wrong in his historical judgment that such thinkers as Aristotle and St. Thomas thought of their own work as "intellectual systems" which might "integrate whole cultural periods." Neither Aristotle nor Aquinas had much success among their contemporaries, and their work presents to the serious student today a record of tentative, dialectical, constantly changing forays into uncharted areas.) But the main point is that Cox now sees metaphysics as a critical enterprise, as the raising of further questions, as the dialectical exploding of presuppositions. The metaphysical impulse is the question-raising impulse.

Moreover, I would like to point out that the empirical

ground which allows men to conceive of the "absolute future" or of an "open future" is precisely the human ability to ask ever future questions. The point of the expression "absolute future" or "open future" is that such a future cannot be conceived merely as a projection from present conditions; for a merely projected future is limited and does not represent the complete realization of historical possibility. Man is gifted with an imagination and a skeptical attitude which make it possible for him to *alter* the conditions of the future, to *change* the world. Consequently, the human animal "transcends" even his own empirical projections: he calls them into question.

How, then, does a man know *now* that his authentic goal is the absolute future, not merely a projection? He cannot envisage an absolute future; all he can envisage is the projected future. He knows that his goal is the absolute future because he recognizes in himself a capacity to change direction, to shift his presuppositions, to imagine new alternatives: in short, to raise limitless series of questions. Right now, this minute, a man can become aware, at least indirectly, of the profundity and limitless resourcefulness of his drive to ask questions. There is no point in history at which he can imagine himself refusing to ask questions, surrendering his capacity to imagine, project, and break out anew. The ground of the conception of the absolute future is man's unrestricted drive to ask questions, his relentless openness.

This is the point of the question—a traditional one—put to the Marxists at the Salzburg Colloquy by J. B. Metz: "Will the realization of the total man give the final answer to man's questions, or will man, when fully developed, be still more the questioner, more capable still of an ever-expanding future? Will the future be filled with questions which exceed and transcend our projects and our tentative notions of the future? This would in no way contradict the autonomy of the human race, since it is this openness to the future which constitutes the very essence of man."

Without the drive to ask questions, revolution, reform, and progress are inconceivable. In order for a revolution to be launched, men must question the present and diagnose it; question other possible alternatives and imagine a new world; raise questions in others until a new community takes shape; and question alternative strategies and tactics for realizing the new against the inertia of the old. A theology of revolution depends at each step upon the relentlessness and the skills of the drive to ask questions. Of course, it is not enough to ask questions; one must also make decisions and, above all, act. But it is useful to notice the fundamental role of question asking in intelligent social and political action.

Moreover, it seems to me that the drive to ask questions is at one and the same time the source of man's openness to God and the source of social and political change. In brief, there is a startling unity between language about God and language about social and political reforms. The human drive to ask questions constitutes the openness which allows men to transcend the present, and gives rise to both languages. To think of the drive to understand as the generator of religious language is, of course, continuous with some strands of tradition; but it is mature to recognize one's continuity with the past.

What is new is the suddenly acquired power of men to change their environment, both natural and institutional. Whereas in earlier days the panorama of human life seemed to confirm that there is nothing new under the sun, nowadays the pace and scope of change are so obvious that someone might plausibly wonder whether there is anything stable. In a world now conceived as a bundle of loose ends, open to the most surprising, contingent, and unpredictable developments—a world of probabilities rather than of certainties—man's sense of responsibility for his values, his actions, and even his survival has become a sign much more cogent as an image of God than the ancient sense of dependence on the God of the ordered cosmos.

In short, theology grows out of reflection upon actual human experience in the world. The experience which captivates the imagination of our age is the experience of change, the move towards further frontiers, the hope of a human brotherly world civilization. In *every* human experience, the language of transcendence is available to men because the human drive to raise questions is present in every experience. It is not necessary to kick the faces of those who preceded us in order to speak of transcendence in our own way. When Heidegger used the language of anxiety and concern, he spoke to the experience of a dying civilization. The God spoken of as *will be* happens to speak more clearly to us, but we are not, except momentarily, at the apex of the human race.

Recognizing that fact, we do not think of God as one on whom we "depend" but rather as one who eludes our attempt to speak adequately of him, even as he eluded the clutches of our ancestors. Taking up our daily, concrete responsibilities, we cannot be sure that we hold God in our hands. Like the atheist, we work in darkness regarding God. But we accept the symbol of the community of truth, freedom, love, and justice bequeathed us in the gospel of Jesus Christ and interpret our labors in its light. If we are correct, God is the one who is now with us without revealing himself magically, and the one who, in the absolute future, will be all in all.

11. Green Shoots of Counter-Culture

The high condition of civilization to which man may attain in the future is almost impossible for us now to appreciate. We can best obtain an idea of it by a comparison of our present condition with that of preceding generations. Nor have we to look very far back. A few years ago, within the memory of a majority of the adults here present —in these United States, whose very existence as a nation was justified by an inspired declaration of human inalienable rights—over four million of human beings were held in slavery by mere might. A majority of the people of our country were at that time fully persuaded that the right to ownership of human beings exists by a law which it was bound to sustain by force if necessary.

We believe that a wise system of education will develop a future civilization as much in advance of that of the present as ours is in advance of the condition of the savage. We may always advance towards the infinite . . .

Address of Senator Leland Stanford
for the opening of Stanford University,
October 1, 1891.

1.

Over the gates of paradise, deputies report, are inscribed the words: "ABANDON REVOLT ALL YE WHO ENTER HERE." Such words guard the portals, now, of California's state universities. Meanwhile, at Stanford, a private school, groves of ancient eucalyptus and thick, frondy palms rise into the mild air, and broad porticoes around the brownstone quad afford protection from the soft December rains. As in Eden, so at Stanford: a mythical tall tree stands in the center, the famous red *palo alto* inscribed on university equipment, on the pull-over of a passing coed, on the marching band's brass drum. This tree has become the symbol of revolt, a revolt all the more fascinating because Berkeley, an hour away across the shimmering Bay, has momentarily gone as limp as a protester with a cop's hands upon his wrists—or else has merely gone underground, quietly building an ever stronger and more disciplined radical base.

Stanford was not founded as a school where the American revolution might be renewed; it has from the beginning been establishment. "Stanford believes," *The Trustee's Manual* tells us, "that education is a prime national asset." From the Founding Grant of Governor and Mrs. Leland Stanford in 1891 until the present, Stanford has overcome great reversals and advanced steadily, often heroically, to a position of eminence next to that of Berkeley and Harvard. It stands now upon the brink of securing a position as one of the few universities in the world to which the word "great" may, without embarrassment, be applied. It has pioneered in developing—on the great plain beneath the blue foothills—the concept of a military-industrial-university complex. "For seventy years," Herbert Hoover wrote, "Stanford University has poured out a glorious stream of youths competent to meet the needs of our growing country and our way of life." The Founding Grant announced of the university: "Its object, to qualify its students for personal success, and direct usefulness in life."

By 1968, however, there were students at Stanford bitterly offended by the very achievements of which administrators and alumni are proud. "*We have been pioneers in creating a new type of community,*" said Provost Emeritus Frederick E. Terman in 1965, the man probably most responsible for Stanford's growth since World War II,"—*one that I have called a 'community of technical scholars.' Such a community is composed of industries utilizing highly sophisticated technologies, together with a strong university that is sensitive to the creative activities of the surrounding industry. This pattern appears to be the wave of the future.*" On a mild April 11, 1967, as if goaded by these words (reprinted prominently on campus in February), students put up harsh posters and sponsored a lengthy parade announcing "WE ACCUSE!"—we accuse, the bearded and unbearded said, Stanford University of immense complicity in making the United

States of America into a repressive, counter-revolutionary, and militarist nation. The protesters presented a long list of industries in the Stanford Industrial Park and their contributions—in dollars, in research, and in products—to present U.S. wars. Stanford's eminence, they argued, is based upon imperialism, naked and undisguised.

There were in 1968 two ways of viewing Stanford—proudly as a saga of success wrested from defeat, difficulties, and disaster, a testament to the great American Dream; and bitterly, as a saga of growing violence abroad and identification with the interests of the wealthy and powerful at home, the *other* testament to the American Dream. No one denies that Stanford is a great, or almost great, university. But some thought of the form of that achievement as a fulfillment, and others as a betrayal.

To see whence we have come, a flashback to the beginnings of the counter-culture may be clarifying.

2.

"Welcome to Santa Clara County: 5000 Ph.D.'s live here," reads the billboard on route 101, twenty-two miles south of the San Francisco airport. In a relaxed-busy way, Stanford is a fascinating mix of Western establishment and Eastern intellection. Its ring of nearly three hundred industries, discreet and neatly lawned, attends the national interest in a way comparable only to the ring of intelligence bounded by route 128 in Massachusetts. Stanford's engineers, lawyers, doctors, physicists, and advisers to the federal government spend hours on long-distance lines and days on airplanes. On the other hand, life in the fence-hidden homes of Portola Valley, Menlo Park, Palo Alto, and Sunnyvale is less frenetic and less grubby than in the East —the good Californian lives with one hand upon the rudder of ease, close to vintage wines and a crackling fireplace, his calendar blocked for trips to the sea or the Sierras. For sheer quality of life—for eating, drinking, loving, playing—California is incomparable. For a natural integrity and innocence and openness to the life of the spirit, California is fresh and alive in ways the East cannot approach. It is, perhaps, the Freudian-

Franciscan utopia Herbert Marcuse and Norman O. Brown sometimes write about; it produces "the Algerian man," the bronzed "man of the noonday sun," Albert Camus celebrated in the last pages of *The Rebel*—the man the history-building Northern European (read Easterner) knows not of.

It is difficult to make clear to Easterners, particularly to well-educated Easterners, what to make of the restless spirit of California. Reagan and the Right Wing complicate the picture; California politics have an exuberance and dash and primitive multiplicity that short out sober minds programmed to the realism of the East. Regularly the mass media and the slick magazines fly bright young reporters out to California on foreign assignment and they come, wearing button-down collars and making the quietly ironic, self-distancing quips that ivy league schools have isolated as the sign of intelligence. They come, they see, they do not understand—and in their tasteful prose California is once more portrayed as playground, carnival, and land of untutored sentiment. Intellect, you would think, has fled California, or never arrived.

Freshmen at Harvard change dramatically in the first six weeks; you watch them, day by day, learning how to say bright things without quite committing themselves, ever guarded, schooled by recent wounds to introduce into their speech ironic detachment, a certain space from which retreat or counterattack may be dispatched. The East educates by detaching the analytic from the affective powers, and honing the former—the imagery of sword and scalpel ("penetrating," "slashing," "laying bare") dominates Eastern academe. Once the mind has been ground, treated, and stropped to the required super edge, it has normally been spoiled—the direct, sentimental, affective, open sides of human life become suspect.

Less than a third of Stanford students come from homes East of the Rockies. Unspoiled by too much tradition, bright without having read nearly as many words as Eastern students, unfamiliar with the Eastern journals, the Stanford student makes discoveries for himself and tastes often the joy of fresh appropriation. He does not know, or care, that in some Eastern schools his joyous discoveries would be taken for granted. Eastern students who encounter new ideas have often, it seems, the feeling that one more piece of sophistication has been added to their armor; they are merely catching up. Eastern students seem more attuned to picking up signals from professional circles and journal articles; Stanford students are freer to be absorbed with their own development, from insight to insight, change to change.

Although as bright as Harvard students, Stanford students do not work as hard (but account should be taken of the rigors of the Stanford quarter system, and the absence of the Harvard "reading period" in January and May). Stanford students do not read as much. More often they take a day to drive out into the mountains or down to the white-cresting sea. They spend more time outdoors, talking or playing basketball (one out of every two Stanford men earned a letter for athletics in high school, along with his A-average). In Cambridge, the grey winter comes in November and the dirty snow still lines the Charles in early April: what can one do but gallop through another hundred thousand lines of print? The Harvard mind is more linear than the Stanford mind.

Consequently, words like "hippie" and "New Left" have a different meaning in the East than in California. To be a hippie is understood, at Stanford, as an accomplishment of spirit and attitude; many students who do not wear beads, sandals, or gold-rimmed glasses have broken from the Protestant ethic of their affluent and generally conservative homes. Many have acquired a freedom of spirit and a sense for acute personal integrity that their pragmatic parents simply cannot comprehend. Many have overcome the reticence, the distance, the make-believe relationships fostered by the Anglo-Saxon commercial (and philosophical) tradition; they do not, indiscriminately, "love everybody" but they do understand that "the flower children" are on to something real, valuable, and woefully neglected in American life: the ability of human beings to be open to one another. To learn such a skill is, in America, like learning to walk again, after a long convalescence of limbs that had lost their life.

3.

Many things make Stanford unique among all the universities of the land. The blue foothills which rise to the West make their first tentative upward sweeps on the eight-thousand acre farm which the Stanfords decided to make the site of a memorial to their sixteen-year-old son, dead suddenly of typhoid on a trip to Italy in 1889. The bereaved parents visited the presidents of Cornell and Harvard, asking advice about a fitting memorial. The prospect of a university, such that "the children of California will become our children," won out. "It will require at least thirty million dollars," they were warned at Cornell. Mrs. Stanford looked at her husband, whose railroad had daringly linked California to the East, and said quietly, "I think we can manage that."

From the great white house of former President Hoover, now the residence of Stanford's president, one views with admiration the red-tiled university amid the palms and the slender Hoover Tower ("phall sym" to the students in their abbreviated designations, and home of an institute for the study of war and revolution, in the cause of peace). Beyond the university and the dark groves of trees that separate the university from public view lies Palo Alto, faintly Mediterranean and yet clearly American in line, and then the quiet blue finger of the Bay. The air is still and soft, carrying barely a suggestion of the sea from over the foothills to the rear. Often one can see the distant fog curling down the Bay from its entrance through the Golden Gate Bridge 40 miles to the north. The fog is seldom propelled as far as Palo Alto, and the clear cobalt days sometimes come linked, like rosary beads, in chains of fifty. The lemon trees bloom just when the evening weather report is describing the first heavy snows to the East. Spring arrives in the last week of January, and in February the campus is in full, sweet flower.

In this paradise, fifty-eight percent of the undergraduates have parents who earn at least $15,000 a year, and half of these earn over $25,000. The families are largely on the Protestant side (sixty-two percent), with Catholics representing fifteen percent (as against twenty-six percent in other secular universities), and Jews only seven percent (as against 18 percent in other private universities and nine percent in all universities). There are, all told, almost twelve thousand students, of whom almost half are undergraduates, in a cruel ratio of one girl for every two boys. One out of every four undergraduates comes from a private high school. Four out of every five go to graduate school. Of the rest, a larger proportion than in any other school enter the Peace Corps.

Stanford is especially proud of having drawn faculty members from ivy league institutions, and legions of graduate students with them. Berkeley sends more graduate students than any other school (274 between 1963 and 1966), but Harvard (172), M.I.T. (156), Yale (127), and Princeton (113) follow in line. Those who know the energy and brilliance of the great creative engineer and former Provost "Fred" Terman will not be surprised to find that, in the annual graduation parade, almost one-fifth of all recipients of Stanford degrees are engineers. Hewlett and Packard are both Stanford men; so was Russell Varian. Among *Fortune* magazine's top 500 business executives, Stanford ranked third as *alma mater* claimed. It was in the Stanford medical school, standing by for months, that history's second successful heart transplant was performed. The two-mile linear accelerator slicing through the foothills gives Stanford physicists one of the greatest scientific instruments in the world. Prizes and fellowships fall on Stanford (faculty and students) more abundantly than on all but two or three schools in the land.

4.

Most of this, fund-raising literature could—and does—make plain. The most important story at Stanford, however, has not been told: of the quiet, steady, and surprising emergence of a small group of radical, even revolutionary, students and their enormous impact upon the life of a majority of Stanford undergraduates. It is among the children of the affluent, the children of professional and successful people, as studies by Katz, Sanford, Flaks, and others show, that radical students tend to come. Thus it is not, after all, amazing that Stanford students seemed to outnumber Berkeley students at the week-long demonstrations at the Oakland induction center in October 1967 (at least on the non-violent days), and that more persons from Stanford were arrested at follow-up demonstrations in December than from anywhere else but Santa Cruz. The national movement "from protest to resistance" seems to have received a major impulse from Stanford initiatives following the scandously poor performance by Vice President Humphrey on the campus in February 1967. And for two years in a row, Stanford students have elected avowed and open "radicals" as student-body presidents; both of whom, to be sure, resigned before their terms were out.

Stanford has not had a tradition as a liberal, still less a radical, school. The first president of Stanford, David Starr Jordan, was an early "dove" and left Stanford in 1913 to lead a national protest against the growing war fever in America and particularly the growing efforts to turn the university "into an adjunct of the war department." But the same President had also presided over the dismissal of Professor Ross in 1903, because that gentleman had voiced political views intolerable to Mrs. Stanford—an action which blotted the young university's academic reputation for many years. The presence of Herbert Hoover, one of the earliest and most illustrous graduates, still lingers. "Personal success," "a useful life," "a practical sense" —to use phrases which recur in early addresses by both Senator and Mrs. Stanford—long seemed to be the marks of a Stanford education. Until relatively recently, strict provisions against "political advocacy" (and against religious sectarianism) governed the spirit, if not the entire practice of campus life.

In 1964, the *Stanford Daily* endorsed Goldwater for president. Polls, however, indicated that sixty-two percent of the students supported Johnson, even though fifty-one percent described themselves as generally "conservative" and leaned towards more liberal Republicans like Rockefeller and Nixon. In 1966, the year of the election of David Harris as student-body president, about a third of the students described the tone of the student body as "predominantly liberal," while an equal number described it as "predominantly conservative." Revealingly, conservatives found it liberal, liberals conservative. Feelings were, however, already tipping the scales in the more liberal direction—a radical minority was beginning to register an intense dissatisfaction which had no conservative counterbalance, and a restless liberal-conservative consensus held that "the administration" was more conservative than the student body. Both conservatives and liberals expressed satisfaction with the faculty, yet in a fashion which led one researcher [1] to conclude that Stanford students had not yet learned to criticize their professors.

How, then, the metamorphosis?

5.

Biographies of students differ, but in interviews conducted in in the early spring of 1968 some patterns begin to emerge. Again and again students mention: the influence of two or three young residence deans of several years ago (Al Lowenstein, later with A.D.A., for example); the influx of graduate students—who become teaching assistants and house residents —from better schools; the experience of living in another country (over half of the undergraduates spend at least two quarters at one of Stanford's five overseas campuses); Mississippi summer in 1964, and the arrival of Robert McAfee Brown, whose intense social concern matched that of the students, in the religion department; the gradually spreading impact of the Peace Corps and of Dwight Clark's Volunteers in Asia, which introduced scores of Stanford students to a summer in the slums of Hong Kong and the villages of Vietnam; the founding of The Experiment and the Free University; the David Harris campaign of 1966; the Humphrey debacle of 1967; and the confrontation with the Oakland police the following October.

Inversely, the figure whom militant conservatives single out with most virulence is Dean of the Chapel, B. Davie Napier,

[1] See Joseph Katz, ed., *Growth and Constraint in College Students,* Institute for the Study of Human Problems (Stanford, 1967).

who came to Stanford in 1966 from Yale, where he had been fellow and then master of Calhoun during eighteen years. A gentle, vulnerable, sensitive man in his early fifties, Napier speedily became one of the best informed persons on the campus, trusted entirely by students and (at first) administrators. He has had the courage to preach a genuine, socially conscious Christianity. The once almost empty campus church, its design a testament to the centuries of Mrs. Stanford's taste and its services long directed mainly at alumni-citizens of Palo Alto, has once again become a student church, a crowded student church. As if in reply, two conservative campus papers soon chose to make Napier the chief target of their maiden numbers; a long and insulting column by the *Daily's* house conservative followed. Administrators—at least one is known by students to hate Napier's views with a passion—and members of the Board of Trustees then began to register stiff, occasionally tasteless complaints. So long as the chapel by its silence blessed the status quo, there is no record of conservatives crying for "neutrality"; but even now some who do not go to church wish to protect God from hearing talk of politics and culture.

Paul Goodman has noted the surprising role of campus ministers in today's radical movements. The ministers surrounding Napier—Richard Roe, Stuart McLean, Barbara Troxell, to name some of the most active—were dependable allies in many campus battles. Yet if Napier, above all, has given prophetic criticism (his scholarly field is Old Testament studies, although he is not now teaching classes) legitimacy on campus, it was here before he arrived. His chief effect, however, seems to be upon the moderate and the respectable. Few radicals learn their stringent code of sanctity from the church, although many come to Napier when they need help—names on a petition, support from an official, an honest counsel, a sounding board for plans. Napier's annual talk to the freshmen during orientation week has become one of the most sensitizing and—in a preparatory way—radicalizing moments of the year. He has shown that religious symbols used with fidelity and courage still have extraordinary social power. But the sources of radicalism at Stanford are mainly secular.

6.

Barry Greenberg, twenty-seven, a graduate student in political science, is not a typical Stanford student. He is not a typical radical, either. He is not even a highly charismatic leader, or the major spokesman for the many radical movements on campus. Some who admire him most agree that he is not always able to communicate his own feelings and ideas to others, even in small and select groups. Yet Barry (no one refers to him as "Greenberg") is one of the most striking leaders to be found in radical circles around the country. He is unusually sensitive to other human beings, and has a penetrating, disturbing interest in political theory. For him theory is genuine only if lived; it is "false consciousness" not to act according to one's theories. He will tell you quietly and seriously that he considers himself a revolutionary—he listed "revolutionary" as his profession in signing the registration form for the Peace and Freedom Party. (The California registrar did not accept his form; revolution is not, apparently, a recognized profession in the state.)

Like a great many Californians, Barry was not born in California. He grew up on Long Island and was a member of a tough and well-armed juvenile gang. When he was still in high school, his father, a jeweller, had had enough of the rigors of New York and moved his family to Los Angeles. Barry went to a high school that prepared those who would not go to college for a trade. The most natural step for a tall, broad, tough, patriotic American boy after such a preparation was the one Barry almost took: he tried to join the Marines. Instead, a watchful uncle talked Barry into attending one of the less distinguished junior colleges, and succeeded in getting him to join the staff of the school paper. Barry, his natural talent suddenly blossoming, took over the sports page; then he became editor. A strange passion was awakened: a questioning attitude.

Barry transferred to Stanford, worked hard, edited the *Daily*, and proceeded steadily into graduate school; he is married and is now the father of a little girl, age seven. Heading towards September 1966, his thesis (on Sartre and Camus) not quite completed, he accepted a handsome offer from a midwestern university. Then just before classes were to begin, the astonished chairman of the midwestern department (and former director of a CIA project in Vietnam) received a letter from Greenberg saying that "in conscience" Barry could not accept the appointment after all, please excuse him, his responsibilities lay with building up "radical community" in the Bay Area. An "existential decision" had been made: Barry had decided to commit his life, not to a Ph.D. and "working within the system," but to revolution.

How does a revolutionary support himself? He must be satisfied with very little; consumer goods, concern for his "standard of living," an itch to possess property, and too many comforts are enemies. Which is why the United States is hardly, Barry notes, a revolutionary country: a man's loyalty to the regime is secured, not by secret police, but by a high standard of living. Barry and his wife Marilou have lived in graduate housing and in an apartment in East Palo Alto (which at least twice has been broken into and robbed of record player, radio, and other moveables). They dress simply and plainly, neither in the ostentatious poverty of Franciscans nor in the uneven prosperity of graduate students. Marilou has taken numerous part-time jobs; Barry has had teaching fellowships at Stanford and later at the Free University of Palo Alto. Since June of 1967, *The Mid-Peninsula Observer,* a radical bi-weekly newspaper founded and edited by Barry, David Ransom, and several others, has found enough financial support to maintain its editors on fifty dollars a week. The paper covers the trials of draft resisters, demonstrations, the struggles of the East Palo Alto black community, and evidences of "university complicity" in the American social-political system. It prints matters that do not appear in the Palo Alto *Times.*

7.

Fifty percent of the undergraduate men at Stanford belong to fraternities. They differ, on the whole, from other groups "in their appearance, interests, and attitudes towards group activities." [2] The impression they give is one of self-confidence, athletic grace, and social attractiveness. They are not strong in self-analysis, but, concomitantly, have the capacity to make quiet and clear decisions; they dislike complexity and introspection. A large proportion aim for managerial and administrative positions; for careers in business and law, rather than in scholarship, the arts, or the professions. Most like the company of other men, rate security high on their list of values, and need a strong sense of loyalty and belonging. The fraternity men represent a deep strain in the American character, and have a natural affinity to university administrators and the majority of Stanford alumni. It is probably significant, then, that the Stanford fraternities are now in turmoil.

Each year, it seems, freshmen take the fraternities less seriously. Several Stanford chapters, moreover, have had serious disagreements in recent years with their national chapters; some have disaffiliated. Beta Chi has a reputation as one of the most stimulating and critical housing groups on the campus. In many respects, however, the fraternities keep alive at Stanford the flavor "of the good old days." The pacesetters in the fraternities come from white Anglo-Saxon homes; their parents hold positions of affluence and influence. These "inheritors" provide models for the rest of the boys; and they exhibit great admiration for their fathers. The Katz study describes these fathers as "above the layer of management where conformity and depersonalization is evident and their strength seems to lie in their capacity to understand different points of view, make clear-cut decisions, and assume responsibility for them." The boys admire their fathers, and yet feel a certain distance from them—their fathers were often away from home. A country club atmosphere, heavy drinking, an executive position, a logical and hardheaded mind, an interest in his boy's achievements, enthusiasm for sports, a nostalgia for college: thus is father evoked. Mother is usually spoken of with affection and condescension, as tolerant and maybe bright, but incapable of objective and balanced opinions. Sixty-eight percent of the fraternity boys describe themselves as being drunk "more than once" during the past year. Their

[2] For a social-scientific profile, see *ibid.*, pp. 297 ff.

110

model in masculinity seems often to include the conquest of women, contempt for persons who are less attractive, strong, and adventurous than their own crowd, and the condoning of aggressive behavior towards outsiders.

Half the fraternity boys live off campus; these are usually brothers less interested in sports and more interested in parties, travel, and "off-beat" activities—including, sometimes, civil rights and anti-war or conservative political activities. Fraternity presidents, meanwhile, are sensitive to the charge that selective rush results in a homogeneity harmful to education; and frequently professors are invited to the fraternities for dinner and a "short, informal conversation," since a new campaign is being launched "to destroy the image that fraternities are anti-intellectual." In 1965 one fraternity admitted girls as associate members; the next year, one voted—and received administration approval—to allow girls to reside on one floor. There are frequent faculty-student discussions on campus about doing away with "the ding" (blackballing of pledges), and opening more and more of Stanford housing units, including fraternities, to coed living. In 1968 as many as half of Stanford undergraduates were living in coed houses.

8.

Paul Rupert turned down Yale and Harvard to come to Stanford from Boston in 1962, and promptly joined ROTC. He was proud when he was accepted at one of the fraternities the following year—the alternative was the one grim residence for upperclassmen, Stern Hall, which at that time was lacking in spirit as much as status. Stern Hall residents tend to be hard workers; a bleak configuration of cement-block boxes, the hall made them feel like Stanford's second best. In his junior year, Paul went off to Italy where he "found himself"; Americans, John Updike has written, receive their supernatural mail on foreign shores. Paul read the liberal journals of his friends, began to read Italian newspapers and saw the war in Vietnam in a new light, did research on the American intervention in the Dominican Republic, and studied the history of the Italian

Communist Party. He wrote later of "beautiful relationships and very full days," and he returned to Stanford "self-critical and critical of my country and my friends as never before."

Before leaving for Europe, Paul had had two powerful experiences. At the beginning of sophomore year, he dropped ROTC because he had found the military "obnoxious and crass," and "didn't want to spend valuable units on map-reading and gun-cleaning." He ran the whole "dating-drinking-cycling" course, and ended the quarter with a 2.4 grade point (4 is maximum), a terrible Christmas, and a desire to start learning. He went to his first Vietnam teach-in as a student cop. He began reading a lot "as I had in high school." He particularly remembers reading Kant on the categorical imperative. In the spring quarter, during rush week, he spent sixteen hours arguing with a Texan in the fraternity who wanted to ding a black whom Paul had worked hard to get to apply. Around and around the argument went, all night. In the end, the Texan admitted that it was sheer prejudice but dinged him. This experience seemed still fresh in Paul's mind when he returned from Italy a year later, and found he "hated the fraternity with a passion."

Like many other newly awakened students, Paul was helped by Professor Helen Schrader of the Communications department, a warm, strong, and penetrating woman whose seminar students learn to speak to one another as human beings, not only as minds. Paul applied to become a sponsor in a freshman dorm, in order to help freshmen "find the strength in themselves that I felt others had helped me to find." He worked for a losing candidate in the primaries for student-body president, and then hesitantly began to work for David Harris, whom he thought to be "a bit radical." The more he saw of Harris, the more he began to examine his own university experience critically. That summer he grew a beard "to show my newly acquired radicalism," read a lot, quarrelled with his parents, and began to write. Returning for his senior year, he gave up his ambition to go to law school, learned to use grass, listened to music more seriously than he had, and went to many films and plays. He developed some "very deep relationships" with Joel

Smith (young and handsome dean of students), David Harris, Dennis Sweeney, Peter Lyman, and other creative and radical students. "I learned more in those nine months than I had in the other three years."

The Humphrey visit to campus occurred when Paul was in the midst "of a very great disillusionment with the university, the country, and the options available for me to live some sort of meaningful life. It really galvanized my political impulses and from that point it became clear that I would spend my life as a teacher-writer-antagonist in an effort to transform this country into something that it certainly was not." He decided that he could not apply for C.O. status but must refuse to co-operate at all. Admitted to the University of Chicago for graduate studies, his induction papers transferred to Oakland, Paul expected to be back in the Bay area early in 1968 "to refuse when it is appropriate."

9.

The election between David Harris and Bob Klein in May 1966 was among the most momentous events in the experience of Stanford students in a great many years. Bob Klein was a well-dressed, clean-cut student who had been president of the political union. A liberal, he urged greater student participation in educational reform, the right to take pass-fail courses outside one's major, and the presence of student advisors on the Board of Trustees. Above all, he urged cooperation and steady progress through normal channels. David Harris, Klein accused, was misled by "pseudo-utopian ideals." No doubt Harris lived by a different style and was a leader of another sort. Blue jeans, old sport coat, Ben Franklin glasses, a frowzy yellow moustache: Harris did not fit the all-American image. Born in Fresno, Harris came to Stanford reading Ayn Rand and fancying Goldwater. But after his freshman year, he went to Mississippi; he saw a good friend kicked and urinated on. He learned something about America. On his return he read Rilke, Lorca, Camus, and other writers. He began to become his own teacher.

Like many others who have traveled his way at Stanford,

Harris volunteered to become a freshman sponsor and saw from a new vantage point the sort of dehumanization a modern university of great cognitive, technical power inflicts on the bright, alert, willing young men who come to it. He did not intend to run for the presidency, but friends persuaded him that fundamental issues were seldom even discussed at the university. Harris agreed on the condition that his platform would demand a revolution in Stanford education. He did not expect—positively did not desire—to win.

The other candidates, especially Klein, wanted to improve the system; Harris wanted to alter it. He wanted a purer form of democracy, with students, faculty, and administration having "one scholar, one vote" in the *election* of the Board of Trustees. Students would regulate their own conduct. All academic requirements except the need for 180 credit units would yield to a system which, for the sake of personal development, would risk "freedom bordering on anarchy." Each person in the university should be an equal to every other, a person, his own chief teacher in a community of inquiry. He wanted changes in one year, not in ten. Klein toured the living groups with a precisely timed schedule; spoke briefly and effectively; moved on. Harris went into the various lounges and sat there casually for hours, taking on all comers in "one to one" sincerity and dialogue.

On a bright, mild May day, 3885 students voted, more than at any time in history. One-third of those who voted for Klein later said explicitly that they were voting against Harris. Only fifty percent of the men and twenty-five percent of the women voting for Klein had positive reasons. Harris' gentle, quiet manner and his authenticity had catalyzed the campus. His ideas demanded profound response from some; but most merely felt the force and power of his life. People had to take sides and Harris himself became the main symbol of the campaign. At issue was a widespread dissatisfaction with the tone and setting of education at Stanford, particularly with the minority status of students. Harris won fifty-seven percent of the vote. A third of those who voted for him considered themselves moderate or even conservative.

The Harris image was a subject of consternation to alumni

and parents; articles and letters filled the air, especially between Southern California and the campus. (Southern California alumni have long been a problem to the administration, which against that backdrop has appeared disturbingly liberal; even in early 1968, President J. Wallace Sterling was defending Stanford against a militantly conservative audience in Los Angeles.) In retrospect, the conservatives were probably right about the impact of this one young man. Probably in no recent period have as many students at Stanford been excited about the question of education, as many arguments and discussions continued, or as many lives been so much altered by one life. A year after Harris left school (without his degree), his impact upon fellow students still came constantly to light. As head of the Bay Area Resistance and member of a nearby commune of like-minded "brothers" (as they describe themselves), Harris awaited government action concerning his refusal to be inducted. He was seen often in the company of Joan Baez. The life-styles of the two of them—the one theoretical, the one affective—seem to coalesce.

10.

The freshmen of 1966 came to a campus at the height of its hope. B. Davie Napier had just arrived. David Harris stimulated the newcomers even more thoroughly than he had reached his fellow upperclassmen. It seemed, for a while, that spirits were so high that many were not walking on the ground. Then a single deed exposed the severe divisions on the campus. On October 20, Dave Harris was walking towards a girl's dormitory for a "hero" party to which each girl had invited "her hero." It was 9:15 p.m., mild and dark. Suddenly thirty or thirty-five fraternity men, wearing halloween masks, jumped him, dragged him into the bushes, taped his legs together and sat on his arms. An extension cord from the dormitory allowed them to plug in a pair of shears and for fifteen minutes they amused themselves shearing his hair down to his scalp. David asked them about their views of themselves and education. They were drawn slowly into a discussion. He asked them to spare his beard; they were nervous about how long it was taking and agreed.

Harris offered no resistance. Later one assailant said: "He really showed the Delts a lot of class. He made us feel sorry we did it." They had shone a light in his face and taken a picture. "Now we'll be proud to have your picture in *Time*," one said. Another said later they did it because they "didn't like the image of Stanford he presented."

Many students (sixty percent in a *Daily* poll) were outraged by the act. Twenty-three percent thought the stunt was "humorous" and seventeen percent would give no direct response. The administration was noisily solicitous. Alumni in certain places seemed to derive from it warm memories of good old days. One alumnus treated the Delts to a steak dinner.

To the more radical students, the incident was a bitter corroboration of the growing divisions in American society. The Stanford Committee for Peace in Vietnam had been founded in the spring of 1965 and had been strong enough to sponsor a march of over a thousand students into Palo Alto—the largest since college liquor regulations prompted the famous "pee-rade" of 1908—to protest the resumption of the bombing of North Vietnam. There was an energetic campaign of rallies and protests in the spring of 1966 but by autumn, the S.C.P.V. was exhausted: the country seemed immovably divided, and the congressional elections of 1966 showed that peace candidates were ineffectual. Despair began to replace hope.

Just after the election of David Harris, the SCPV had played a leading role in the sit-in in President Sterling's office to protest the use of Stanford facilities for selective service examinations. Thirty-nine students tied up the office for fifty hours. The Stanford administration, having observed events at Berkeley, kept cool; Dean of Students Joel Smith was especially decent. President Sterling refused to meet with the entire group; the group was not forced out by the use of police. Slowly the arguments in the group shifted from the selective service exams to a student vote in university affairs.

The Stanford administration has been willing to include student representatives on various committees, on the long-term

Study of Education at Stanford, for example. Many students—budding pragmatists—reacted favorably; steady progress, especially in housing regulations, has been made these last two years. But such discussions, radical students report, begin within a limited context: present funds, present programs, present facilities. The administration thus holds all the cards. Pragmatism rules. Many formerly liberal students have come to see that a reasonable pragmatism is the most effective of tyrants. It depersonalizes. It covers inhumanity with the rhetoric of reason, realism, and even freedom.

The progress of Joel Smith, bright and handsome young lawyer from Minneapolis, strikes many of the radical students as a powerful example of the inadequacies of pragmatism as a way of life. A Marshall Scholar at Oxford for two years, Joel (as many then called him) came to Stanford early in 1965 as an attorney in the General Secretary's office. In the summer of 1965, he was named associate dean of students for student organizations; within a year he was, at thirty-four, dean of students and associate provost. He told the *Daily* in 1965: "I have an ardent philosophical interest in education." For at least a year, no administrator was more of a friend to the students than Joel. Many of the most radical students counted him an ally. At the sit-in, Joel had been willing to do all the negotiating; at all-night vigils in White Plaza, Joel had kept away those who had planned to harass. More than once, radical students warned Joel that a man of honesty and integrity could not keep his job; he would be torn between sympathies for the students and certain higher university officials who regarded students as, at best, necessary evils. Joel replied that he, too, feared such a conflict, but that it had not yet arisen, and that he would quit his job if he was ever forced to compromise his principles.

One student, who was once close to Joel, voices a common view about "what has happened to Joel Smith." It goes: "His legal training gives him a language and a perspective that protects him from moral and political confrontation, and gives him an ideology which he refuses to acknowledge. That ideology stresses power and achievement; these are fundamental to 'realism.'" Key students saw Joel as one who loves to picture himself as "defending their interests": flying to Los Angeles to meet with Joseph Califano, LBJ's aide, on the problems of the dissenting, disaffected college student; flying to Washington to "change the draft laws." They don't admire that path, nor its effectiveness. Some months ago, Barry Greenberg told Joel that he sympathized with Joel in his difficult position between students and administrators. As the story goes—it reflects a dominant mood among liberal and radical students—Joel replied: "Don't feel sorry for me, Barry. I'm the enemy."

11.

The Stanford faculty has been slow to exercise leadership in protesting the war, in criticizing the "channelling" concept of General Hershey's draft system, in facing the dehumanization experienced by Stanford students. Few if any Stanford initiatives came from the faculty—in none of the main issues of the past few years have faculty members taken the lead. The faculty is professionally very able; relations between them and the students are usually warm. And yet professional interests dominate; and professors are by and large too busy in their fields to think of the questions of education, society, and personal life that preoccupy students. The students, even the radical students, have not matured enough to criticize the faculty directly; mostly, one hears words of admiration touched with disappointment: "Where is there any leadership, any leadership whatsoever?" Many students despair of professionalism—and of those other key words of a generation ago: liberalism, pragmatism, realism. The most telling lesson in the bankruptcy of mainstream liberalism, however, was driven home by Vice President Humphrey's shocking performance at Stanford on February 20, 1967.

The campus was preparing for Humphrey's visit for more than a week. At the end of January, a group of students from the ecumenically united religious groups had collected funds to send two professors to the Washington mobilization of the Clergy and Laymen Concerned about Vietnam. They then sponsored rallies in White Plaza and smaller discussions. The radical students were discouraged and relatively quiet. Thus, just as

Humphrey arrived, leadership in the anti-war movement had passed to moderates and newcomers. A faculty committee hastily organized by Professors Mark Mancall (Asian Studies) and Lucio Ruotolo (English) urged as many persons as possible to greet Humphrey in strict silence, wearing white arm bands, and pledged neither to applaud not to boo. Student groups—not consulted about this proposal in advance—held strategy meetings of their own. The radicals had collected a file on Humphrey's speeches and insisted that the Vice President no longer heard alternatives but only emitted propaganda. They were insulted that he was being offered a university platform, in order to lend Stanford's prestige—their prestige—to such propaganda. The moderate students, together with the initial faculty group, argued that militant protests antagonized public opinion. A young man with a soft Georgia accent, who had recently resigned from ROTC, was especially persuasive in arguing that demonstrations should be "effective" and "designed to persuade the uncommitted, not to alienate them." "I know what the people back home think," he said, "when they see pictures of wild demonstrations."

In the end, ecumenism triumphed: all anti-war groups would work together. The night preceding Humphrey's visit, an all night teach-in was held—as usual, all the radical students were there, relatively few moderates. Early the next morning, crowds massed outside Memorial Auditorium. Although students and faculty were admitted one-by-one through a single door, where identity cards were checked, the 1700 seats inside were filled in fifteen minutes; many of the one thousand students and faculty wearing white arm bands and pledged to silence did not get in. (Although official denials were forthcoming, many thought at the time that the auditorium had secretly been packed through other doors.) When Humphrey entered, those in the front rows rose as one man and the ovation of the unpledged overpowered the silence of the pledged. Humphrey began his address to a tense, divided university audience by honoring them with their recent appearance on the cover of *Time* magazine as members of "The Now Generation." His glib, insensitive speech was met with incredulity, then disgust, then outrage by many of those who until this moment had considered themselves moderates.

About sixty radical students rose to walk out just after Humphrey began to speak, to demonstrate that they knew he would voice no honest opinion. Others, persuaded by the moderates, had decided "to give the Vice President of the United States a chance." They sat quietly for almost twenty minutes, while Humphrey evaded the question of the war in his prepared remarks, tried to picture himself as a former radical, and then, when three selected panelists finally brought the question up, spoke of the war in simplicities which well-read students knew were simplicities. When he claimed that the university community supported the administration, almost two hundred others, many of whom had not intended to walk out, rose and quietly filed out. Outside, listening by loud speaker, students and faculty evaluated every sentence and some shouted: "Shame!" or "Lie!" at the succession of simplicities. A serious, reasoned, complex talk about the war would, that day, have persuaded many at Stanford. The anger that Humphrey generated—oblivious to his own ineptitude—turned hundreds of heretofore inactive students into militant opponents of the administration.

Humphrey appeared at a window after the speech. Those outside cried "Shame! Shame!" A crowd gathered to let Humphrey know the insult he had delivered, and to let him feel their detestation of the murder and destruction committed in their name in Vietnam. ("We do not bomb civilians," Humphrey had answered indignantly. "But you can't put a bomb in a barrel.") The secret service whisked Humphrey to his car fifty yards away—students came running to shout "Shame!" and, from the more angry, "Murder!" Two protesters were moved from his unmarked path by police. No one touched Humphrey or his car. The shoving and the running, less rough than in a crowd after a football game, nevertheless conveyed a sense of stampede and an electric passion of outrage. A secret service man kicked over a rancid can of beer and thought someone had thrown a container of urine at him. Humphrey was still speaking bitterly of his Stanford experience a year later.

Worst of all, President Sterling apologized, not to the university for the Vice President's performance, but to Mr. Humphrey for the university's. There had been no violence, no riot, nothing but the excitement of running and voicing "Shame!"—and an utterly shameful bit of government propaganda. President Sterling then took the extraordinary measure of sending a letter to every person at the university "out of a deep concern for the preservation of free and civilized debate." The debate, students felt, had not been free; it was, on Humphrey's part, a mockery of civilized discourse: he was using the platform of a great university to clothe the government's policies with respectability, and there was no provision for genuine cross-examination by the university community—nothing like the freedom of the Oxford Union, for example. The helplessness of the United States Senate regarding U.S. foreign policy was experienced at Stanford that February 20. The moderates felt betrayed. The radicals said: "We told you so."

12.

The vision of radical students, which had begun in hope with the eloquent Port Huron statement of 1962, was at Stanford as elsewhere encountering the ugly realities of American life. Henry Steele Commager has recently written: "What is the silence that has fallen on the leadership of the university—presidents, deans, boards of trustees, and regents alike? . . . from Cambridge to Berkeley, from Madison to Baton Rouge, not a single president of a great university has taken a public stand on what is the greatest moral issue of our time." A managerial society, run by liberal pragmatists, is hell. Some administrators seem to see their task as that of easing conflicts and adjusting tensions. That is not the same as facing issues. Some seem to picture themselves as embattled between the tough, wealthy rhinoceri of the right and the obstreperous, unshaven "fascists" (as at least one has called them) of the left. Radical students do not blame such administrators; even good, humane men are obliged to play roles they do not like. That is the nature of the system they have chosen to serve. Within the narrow bounds in which the pragmatism of power and money constricts them, many sensitive administrators complain that they have little room for the life of the spirit: the very life—of liberty, inquiry, prophetic criticism, humanity, and love—which the university is charged to defend and to expand. The university must present a smooth face to the world: it oils the engines of society; it channels technicians into the work force; it sends out artists and healers to help us adjust to the meanness of life; it is a prime national asset. The university no longer tries to change America into a republic of learning; it has been changed into a tool of America.

The fascination of Stanford is that its radicals spring from an unexpected quarter. Berkeley is attended by students of a far more varied social, economic, and political background; and Berkeley's radicals have a tradition. What is happening at Stanford, as the stories of Paul Rupert and David Harris illustrate, is that a deep restlessness has taken root in the very bosom of the successful middle classes. Stanford is "down-home America" at its best—high school presidents, editors of school papers, valedictorians, athletes from the best suburbs of California and the nation. Moreover, the innocence, honesty, idealism, and initial naïveté of such young people is a tribute to the middle class. Hypocrisy abounds in our society, yet somehow the young are prepared not to accept it as a matter of course but to despise it. When they venture outside the secure ghettos by which their earlier education had protected them from the bitterness of human life in this century, they have the moral resources to be shocked.

The most painful confrontation, however, has not been with right-wing America—with the forces of "law and order" represented in different tones of voice by George Wallace and Ronald Reagan, or even with the fraternity brother and ROTC cadet—but with the liberal professor, administrator, writer, and politician. The liberal does not seem to recognize that old words like "freedom of speech," "responsibility," "compromise," "decorum," and the like no longer mean what they used to mean; the international and national context is different. The forces of violence abroad and injustice at home, exploiting mass communications, are hiding behind liberal phrases—it is the age of doublethink. Neither the CIA nor Dow Chemical has any sacrosanct right to use university facilities for their own internal purposes. At the very least, students who face induction and death in connection with national policies supported by such organizations wish to challenge these recruiters to a debate. At Stanford, on November 1, 1967, a group of faculty and students, having asked the university on October 30 to bar such recruitment, milled around one of many doors to the hall which CIA recruiters were using. Joel Smith asked them to disperse and began writing down the names of persons he recognized. Not all who were present intended to block the door. About twenty persons, newsmen following, climbed up a fire escape and danced and stomped on the floor above the recruiters. The administration professed to see in such a protest an outrageous affront to "freedom of speech," to the "rights of others," and to "good order."

Months later, after lengthy hearings, the student Judicial Council rejected the charges which the administration had brought against nine students out of the hundred demonstrators, on grounds that the university policy on demonstrations was unconstitutional, vague, and unenforceable, and that no violation of the university's Fundamental Standard had taken place. Joel Smith, still intent on "securing a conviction," took the charges to a faculty Judicial Board, but the student Judicial Council refused to release the tapes of the earlier proceedings; and those charged refused to appear. What is most astonishing to radical students, and to liberals on the verge of joining them, is that neither administrators nor faculty re-examined the notion of "freedom of speech." The protesters *wanted* the C.I.A. and Dow to explain themselves. They *wanted* the administration to debate its policies on employment services on campus; for, after all, not every solicitor is provided facilities. The administration publicly questions the "tactics" of the radicals, Their "manner," the "danger" they represent to our "institutions." But it is precisely the tactics, manner, and danger being run by the university and our other "institutions" that the students wish to see publicly debated—in a debate between equals, not between prosecutors and defendants in which only the prosecutors establish the rules. In a pragmatic setting, free speech is a charade; those with power make the important decisions. For the liberal, the separation between thought and action is free speech; for the students (as for Sartre), the separation between thought and action is bad faith.

13.

The fifteen months since the Humphrey speech have been long, hard months for Stanford liberals. The radicalization of more and more students occurs with every fresh event in the chain of absurdity, pose, and half-truth that characterize American political life. In October 1967, more than a thousand Stanford students traveled to Oakland to watch long lines of marching policemen, their feet falling heavily in the street and the sun gleaming from their helmets, moving against fellow students. They saw the naked force on which "law and order" rest, and they saw *whose* law and order it was: cop after cop had a prosperous pot belly and blue eyes, and the plain-clothes inspectors, captains, and F.B.I. photographers wore the same haircuts and suits as congressmen, businessmen, and professors. Several dozen students and two faculty members who sat in spent ten days in the Santa Rita prison in October (some of the girls served out their sentences on weekends), or twenty days in December (when sentences were harsher). They experienced the stupidity, petty cruelty, and viciousness of the county prison system, and became friends with the blacks and the poor who were fellow prisoners.

Like David Harris before him, a sensitive and intelligent graduate student named Peter Lyman was elected student-body president in 1967 on a platform asking for an educational revolution; his emphasis was on "community." Once again, the election resulted in little more than the stimulation of critical faculties among some students; student government has no power, and what is urgent to students is patently a good deal less so to those who wield power. Lyman resigned in the autumn quarter.

Meanwhile, the government began to put Stanford draft resisters in jail. Then the new draft policy, concentrating on this year's and last year's graduating class, showed Washington's contempt for pragmatic administrators and student radicals alike. A war against the American way of life seemed to become more necessary every day. More realistically than a year ago, student conversations turned to the probable guerrilla war in America's cities coming soon and to acts of sabotage. An ROTC building was burned to the ground at Berkeley in February. Within a week, bright flames licked the wooden Navy ROTC structure at Stanford. The arson, officials noted grimly, was skillfully executed. Booklets from Canada explained how to make molotov cocktails, how to use explosives, how to set fires. Students whose humanistic convictions had once made them believe that killing is immoral had been placed in the position of being forced to kill anyway—either in Vietnam or here at home, either Asian peasants or American whites. Most Stanford radicals still appear to be pledged to non-violence; but the number of those who cross over the line towards violence, at first only in principle, seemed for a while to increase monthly.

It is much easier to lecture on Kafka to Stanford students today than three years ago. Madness, nihilism, suicide, revolt are daily, nerve-rending issues. The tortured characters of *The Possessed* no longer seem remote and abnormal. *Catch 22* is today. The choices of Bonhoeffer, Camus, and Sartre against a different sort of tyranny have become models to consider fearfully, because one's life is at stake. Education has become a serious business.

Stanford's tall red tree was once a symbol of serenity and progress. Defoliated, it guards private and communal inferno. Some may perhaps be forgiven if they refuse to peer into the pit awaiting our society. Yet such a refusal is a form of bad faith. And is it not the purpose of a university education to detect and to expel, step by step, every vestige of such faith?

12. The Revolution Is Not on Campus

TEN years ago college kids resented being called kids. Today they call one another kids with pride and solidarity. Today students have power; they do not need to play pretend.

What is happening in the colleges today may be decisive for the next thirty years. Small but articulate groups of students have attained an astute political consciousness and are promising disruption and rebellion. The Congress is threatening reprisal. A nation founded by an armed revolution and still pledging allegiance to unfulfilled revolutionary principles—like liberty and justice for all—does not wish to educate rebellious students.

What, then, is an education for? In the minds of many, a kid who "turns out right" moves into the social network of Ameri can industry with an affable smile, an easygoing manner, and the reliable, efficient, pragmatic style on which our technological society depends. Hardheaded, realistic, and committed to the demands of the present order of things, such a promising young man is encouraged to indulge in sentimentalities about defending freedom.

One sees his friends in Vietnam: crew-cut, clear-eyed, soft-spoken, determined. One sees them everywhere in the universities: clean-shaven, hard-working, bright, smooth. These are the "silent students," not represented by the radicals who dominate the news; for there is nothing new about them. The American educational system has been geared to turning out millions of them.

What is an education for? To keep the clocks ticking, the factories humming, and the planes flying? To keep American democracy strong? To keep the young loyal? To teach them to be happy with bread and circuses?

The liberal answer to that question during the past thirty years has been to use the schools as agencies of progressive political and social enlightenment. And, indeed, public opinion polls regularly show a marked correlation between length of education and progressive views. But the liberal solution was a compromise with the ongoing system. Against utopianism and apocalypse, liberalism under Franklin D. Roosevelt chose pragmatic adjustment from within the system. The fruits have been many. But the compromise appears, now, to have broken down. The evidence is the malaise felt almost everywhere.

The public schools are supported by public money and the private schools are supported by industry and government. How can such schools prepare students to be revolutionaries? How can any system prepare young people to transcend itself? The problem is even more vexing than the problem the institutional church must face: how to catechize prophets. For in the society at large, all the wealth, power, and force of arms of the social system are preserving the system on its present course.

Where revolutionary criticism is neither promoted nor heeded, moreover, those who strike the revolutionary pose for its own sake—desiring neither power nor its responsibilities but inner exaltation—are difficult to distinguish from genuine men of power. Without the hot-blooded, the romantic, and the profoundly confused, on the other hand, no revolution can proceed. A revolution is not an act of reflection but of passion. Tom Paine's instability is not an argument against the validity of 1776, and it is unfair to discredit the present revolution merely by denouncing its tactics or the personalities of some of its leaders.

Do we want a political revolution in the United States, a serious rearrangement of the bases of power, wealth, and prestige? That is the fundamental educational question. If we do not want a serious revolution, then we should allow our various educational systems to function as they are. The logic of such a political choice would lead us to: (a) quash the student revolutionaries forcibly, or (b) co-opt their energies in pseudo-revolutionary programs (place them on committees). Generally, it is the liberal administrator who is the slowest to grasp the force and the origin of such logic. That is why he is the most hateful in the students' eyes.

There has not been much serious revolutionary passion in the U.S. since the days of Reinhold Niebuhr's *The End of an Era*. But the doors of the Pandora's box closed by World War II have again flown open. Can a capitalistic democracy possibly serve the ideals of "freedom and justice for all"? Or is the whole system inherently contradictory?

When young radicals close down one or another university, it would be a mistake to imagine that merely procedural issues are at stake. A streamlining of the administrative process or functional adjustments that relieve the pressure at concrete points of protest will not meet the issue. (In liberal pragmatic theory, issues are swiftly reduced to functional, operational terms.) The revolution that has begun on the campuses is not raising a procedural issue; it is substantive.

That revolutionary issue has two parts. In the first place, the crew-cut, affable American is not always an attractive human type. He may be repressed, empty, quietly and blindly savage, without an interior life, boring and bored. The first substantive issue has to do with inhibitions, repressions, and diminished imaginative and affective capacities.

In the second place, the revolutionary issue is concerned with economics, technology, the mass media, and political machinery. What is good for Texas money does not, clearly, promote "freedom and justice for all." The "law and order" that police forces now defend does cruel and arrogant violence to too huge a number of human beings; it is not tolerable. The interests that dominate social and political decision making in the U.S. are unfaithful to the revolutionary ideals on which this country is founded.

Faced with such a revolution, on whose side are the universities? And do they dare to say so? There is no other basic educational issue.

The issue, while basic, is not, however, simple. The university

128

is an international institution; it is not committed to the self-interest, or even the dominant sense of reality, of any one nation. Its loyalty is to human survival, and to that expansion of liberty which comes from inquiry. A university is not a *direct* revolutionary weapon. It is a gathering place within which revolutionary consciousness may be nourished. But if it becomes involved in direct action against its society, it fights with weapons and skills not really its own or congruent with its own sustained possibilities, and it will surely be crushed by forces far stronger than it is.

The university is a dependent institution. Without a certain affluence, a certain leisure, a certain solution to the fundamental necessities of order and food and housing, universities do not even come into existence. They are a sign of a confident and secure society, strong enough to bear criticism and new perspectives, and wise enough to want them. Usually, of course, societies *say* they want frank and thorough criticism and utterly free inquiry—like wives saying, "How do you like my hair? Be truthful now." One had better be discreet.

Yet in universities more than in any other location in a society we may in a sustained way stand outside the ordinary sense of reality, the accepted story, the key symbols of one's nation. One may attain a critical and revolutionary perspective. One may conceive of programs and devise strategies. But the social, economic, and political *base* of a revolution must, to be successful, be located at a much more central place in the society.

The university in the last thirty years has tended to serve the international interests of the industrial state too uncritically. In so doing, they have served, and helped to create, a new suburban class of technically skilled men. They have not impartially served all men, of all nations. To that extent, they have been unfaithful to man, the planetary animal, all too faithful to the national interests of the United States. Are univeristies free to belong to man, and particularly to the vast majority of men, the dispossessed? May they look at their world through *their* eyes, with their interests also in view? That is the revolutionary contribution of universities. The social, economic, and political base of the revolution is not, however, on the campus—only some breathing space, some room to let one's mind roam, some incentive to think in fresh and uncoerced ways, like Marx in the reading rooms of the British Museum in those vastly fruitful years.

13. Hypocrisies Unmasked

THE radical protests in one after another American university have rendered the empire naked. Almost everyone is embarrassed. Under intense pressure, opposing myths about our society are passionately set forth without their customary clothing. The "end of ideology" has ended; freedom has begun.

The radical left is riven by a split between progressive labor militants and gentler S.D.S. factions who recall the humanism of the Port Huron Statement. Yet even the most gentle have been driven to sickness and despair by their experiences these last three years. "Moderate" students are divided between those who concede the good points raised by the radicals, but still believe that "reason" and "democratic procedures" operate in the universities; and those who rush from fraternity houses to drive the protesters from their sit-ins, or who desire still stronger police retaliation.

The moderates accuse the radicals of infringing on the liberties of the majority. The radicals retort: Can't you see that the liberties of the majority are more apparent than real, infringed on every day by an armed government and by fatally deficient democratic procedures?

The moderates say that they are a majority. They like the Establishment, on whose bottom rungs their feet are firmly placed, the way it is. The radicals retort: Can't you see that the Establishment has bought you off, that you have been channeled into this place, and are being taught precisely those skills the Establishment most wishes you to have? And that other people are dying from the narrowness and inhumanity of those skills?

Newspapers speak of "Reform by Bully." *The New York Times* editorialized: "The nation's leading universities have shown themselves slow learners of a fundamental lesson: Reforms accomplished through surrender by the majority to force and unreason invite the continued exercise of control over campus government by those who know how to coerce and bully." The editors of *The Times* fail to see that "the majority," whether of university students or of American people, have long since "surrendered" to the "force and unreason" exercised by minorities, who under velvet gloves well "know how to coerce and bully." *The Times* is offended by the protests of radicals against the powers-that-be in government, industry, and university—more offended than it is by the "force and unreason" exercised daily by those same powers-that-be.

Prison sentences for those who resist the draft, the "channeling" of one's life by government authorities, the social power of universities to sort out which students will join established elites and which will not, the real estate interests of university corporations, the stranglehold of professional guilds upon what the curriculum will consider real and what unreal, the interests of business and industry in supporting an "objective" methodology that promotes two human capacities, the storage of information and the analysis of information, above all others—all these comprise a partial list of the daily employment of "force and unreason" to which American young people are subjected.

Moreover, professors too have lost their clothes. Some students have long wanted to grill them: "But, professor, what do *you* think?" Many professors consider such a question illegitimate. They do not take the rostrum to expound their own views, to propagandize, to reveal themselves. They are spokesmen for their professional discipline. Students have grown accustomed to such duality—the man as man, the man as mouthpiece —and they no longer admire it. For "the professional discipline," it turns out, also has its own interests, biases, screens, and blindnesses. Industry and government pay it well. Its "objectivity" is in fact a nest of special methods required for a rationalized, centralized, technological, capitalistic society. It is not "objective," but one peculiar way of life, not the most admirable, out of many.

Again, some professors at Cornell have resigned because of the arms carried by black protestors; they did not resign because of the fear under which blacks, even at Cornell, live daily—or over the burning of a cross the night before. They have been shocked by the resistance of blacks to the peculiar patterns of "reasonable discourse," "objectivity," and "democratic procedures" selected by great American universities; they have been less shocked by the exclusion from universities of values, perceptions, attitudes, and methods dear to most peoples of most cultures in human history. Feeling, fantasy, impulse, ritual, prehistoric emotional signals, subtle perceptions in human relations, and the like are systematically excluded from the universities in favor of highly developed and economically productive powers of analytic reason. The universities function to sort out those human types that manifest qualities along one small range of the human spectrum.

At Princeton, spectators are not horrified by the ranks of young men channeled into R.O.T.C. by Selective Service requirements and taught during their university education to bear arms in the defense of empire. They are shocked by the ragged, freely chosen, bitterly hostile, and derisive march of S.D.S. irregulars onto the parade grounds. (Did British soldiers once stand in rank near Princeton, scorned by the rabble?)

At Harvard, a dean of highest stature wrote to President Pusey last February that major resolutions taken by his faculty regarding the R.O.T.C. were "very badly framed, gratuitously unpleasant, and basically confused." He reviewed the President's options and recommended that the faculty be asked to re-write its decision. He describes whatever dissent might arise from the faculty as "loud squeals." He expresses sorrow that the Harvard faculty obliged him to transmit "the quickly formulated product of emotional debate."

A great many persons seem to be shocked that the S.D.S. employed political manipulation in generating the dramatic conflict at Harvard; few seemed shocked by the political manipulation daily practiced by administrators. A protestor at Harvard stole the Dean's letter from a file cabinet and, as he had learned from Washington politics, leaked it to the press. Deplorable actions which observers daily expect from adults shock them in students.

In a word, the liberal, reasonable, "objective" character of academic freedom is shown by events to be not only "fragile and delicate" but rather more apparent than real. Young men feel inexorable curtailments of freedom. Not all points of view are welcome or even expressible under the approved conditions and methodologies. The liberal, reasonable men who lead universities, and who teach at them, must take swift steps to overcome their fey revulsion and to open their eyes to a world they are unaccustomed to seeing. Their tactics of close conversation; prolonged openness; hard, honest public debate; and a willingness to confess the partiality and relativity of one's own methods are more proper to universities than swift, fifteen-minute assaults by club-swinging police.

The temperature of radicals, moreover, is uncontrollably high. From their point of view, the issues are life or death. But a serious revolution requires ice in the veins. Repetitive theater is not only boring; it calls forth hoots and jeers.

On some campuses, the time is ripe for public debates between radicals and liberals, in which each participant can choose his own style. (For the present style of "objective" debate is prejudiced in favor of the technological, analytic way of life.) In many other places, the dominant liberal complacency is so strong that unless its nakedness is demonstrated the issues cannot be intelligently discussed. In such a place, dramatic pressures may still be needed.

Radicals need to know that if force arouses counterforce, they are the weakest party. It is not wise to commit all one's resources in the beginning.

14. The Realists and the Radicals

ALL GREAT revolutions in moral values, in politics, and in the humanities hinge upon new definitions of "reason." Thus all such revolutions have the aspect of struggles between fundamental myths. They cannot be resolved by appeal to or in the name of reason. For contrasting conceptions of reason are what the struggle is about.

Each new revolutionary elite seems irrational and dangerous by the standards of the former custodians of the reasonable; each former establishment seems dogmatic, rigid, and narrow by the standards of the revolutionaries. Since reason alone, therefore, cannot be the instrument of adjudication, a period of revolution in moral values, and in the conception of politics, and the humanities, appears to be "a darkling plain, where ignorant armies clash by night."

By now, no one connected with lively college students can doubt that the intellectual orientation, methods, attitude, style, standards, and procedures that have for generations governed academic life in America—traditions inherited from Greece and Rome, from Judaism and Christianity, from the Enlightenment, and from the spectacular explosion of the natural and social sciences in the last fifty years—are considered too narrow, dogmatic, rigid, and (above all) untrustworthy by many of our very best students.

It is no mere social or political revolt we now experience. The struggle is not for more lenient parietal hours, or for increased participation in administrative power; the struggle is over a new theory of the intellectual life, a new definition of reason, and a new conception of the humanities.

And the enemy in this struggle, the enemy of the students, will

135

increasingly be seen to be, not the administration, but the faculty. The administration may be the guardian of functional necessities; but the faculty is the guardian of the prevailing myth by which reality is to be perceived; the prevailing definition of reason, method, argumentation, and even perception. What the faculty says is important *exists;* what the faculty ignores *does not exist.* Realism is what one learns in college.

But many students are listening to new voices, suppressed voices, gravely suspect voices. And they are grappling for a fresh theory of the intellectual enterprise that would allow them to legitimize those voices, to let them be heard in the arena of debate, discrimination, and distinction. They will not be put down by accusations of irrationality, romanticism, fantasy, or fascism. They have been stirred by such voices; they know that they are on to something real.

If the intellectual establishment cannot absorb these darkly sensed realities into their own frame of reference without distortion, then so much the worse for traditional frames of reference. The events through which young people have lived since 1959 —particularly those who have been bright, sensitive, and involved since the age of twelve—have been so bitter, absurd, painful, mad that their experience simply cannot be contained in the categories of American academic life. Realistic, pragmatic, empirical language is too constricting for the human experience in our time. A more adequate language is yet to be found.

In such a context, those whose profession is ethical reflection must grapple afresh with the Christian realism enunciated so forcefully by mentors like Reinhold Niebuhr, whose stature they cannot hope to rival, and with the parallel realism of Hans Morgenthau, George Kennan, and others. The main struggle of these twin realisms was against an idealism that was at once moralistic, individualistic, and isolationist. The international context in which these twin realisms were born was that of nation states at the height of their ambition, power, and unquestionable status as foci of community values. Technology was not then so advanced as to have established a single network of worldwide communication. The international habit of mind was only just beginning to be implanted: the habit of mind that sees in virtually every revolution, riot, or provocation anywhere in the world the threat of involving the two great power blocs that stand astride the globe. An international culture of music, dress, restiveness, and reaction against pragmatic politics had not yet taken hold among the world's youth. The perception of race and poverty as international problems was not widespread.

In brief, both the ideological enemy and the global situation that gave rise to realism were different from the enemy and the context of today. It should not surprise us, then, that the terms of ethical argument once so prominent—interest, power, prudence, hardheaded analysis, national community, pragmatism—have a different ring today. Not everything is different, and hence some of the hard-won wisdom embodied in realism remains valid, and some of its methods, distinctions, and operations retain at least some of their power to persuade.

\ On the other hand, loaded words like "revolution" and "radicalism" have the power \ to move many persons today to fresh analyses they might not otherwise have made, and also the power to disturb and even anger other persons; just as loaded words like "immoral society," "the myth of original sin," and "dialectic" had similar power a generation ago. Then as now the new sources of analysis were deemed irrationalist, destructive, negative, and uncivilized.

The key symbol to be redefined, then as now, is "reason." Against the rational, logical, structural "reason" of idealism, whether of the scientific or of the moralistic sort, realism argued for hardheaded, concrete analysis of the factors of power and interest, and for functional adjustments aimed at restoring, not some ideal utopia, but a delicately counterbalanced equilibrium poised over a larger chaos. Today, it is the myth of hardheadedness that is under attack, as well as the adequacy and depth of functional analysis.

As culture interacts with culture, and as the analytic reason of the Western tradition comes to be heard as but one voice in a worldwide chorus, differences in perception, viewpoint, perspective, and self-definition have become increasingly significant variables in political and ethical discourse. It becomes apparent that "facts" are not nearly so "hard" as our prejudices would like them to be—that "facts" are determined by the qualities of perception and understanding put into the questioning that isolates them in the stream of human experience.

Similarly, "trends" are estimated differently by observers whose sense of history and of the future are in disagreement.

Finally, "desired outcomes" are defined quite differently by persons who have opposed views on what it is that makes a man a man. The four negotiating partners at the Paris peace talks differ regarding their views of facts, trends, and desired outcomes; their interpretations of what is actually happening in Vietnam is "worlds" apart.

The political and ethical language of the future must be more internationalist than the categories of realism. For realism is a peculiarly Western approach to human experience. The "revolution" spoken of by today's radicals is not only a change in social and political strategy, but also a change in psychic orientation. "Consciousness" replaces "analytical reason" as the basic category of inquiry. Myth and symbol, feeling and fantasy, experience and imagination, sensitivity and sensibility, are given an explicit role in the expression of ethical and political perception and action.

What realists find romantic, irrational, self-indulgent, and the like are regarded by radicals as basic and inalienable factors in ethical and political transactions. Radicals would like to take careful and detailed cognizance of such factors. They do not believe that the categories of realism exhaust the relevant or even the important factors in ethical and political inquiry. In this sense, radical thinkers are concerned to enlarge the range of basic terms, the analytic operations, and the context of ethical and political discussion. They do not so much repudiate realism as transform it by enlargement.

It is characteristic of young men, however, to assert themselves at the expense of those from whom they have learned most, and of whom they are most in awe. Such assertion, like adolescence, passes.

The future lies in wedding the realism of the liberals to the imagination of the radicals. An enlarged realism will assure that good inspirations be translated into political fact. A chastened imagination will assure that "political facts" be understood in a more humane and self-critical light.

15. The Volatile Counter-Culture

By invading Cambodia and referring to students, just after the Kent State killings, as "bums," President Nixon gave the radical movement a new lease on life; the movement depended on him for its life. For one of the most important features of the counter-culture is its volatility; it constantly takes new directions, abandons old heroes, seeks new excitement. To clarify this point, we may distinguish three elements: the youth culture, the movement, and radical politics.[1]

The youth culture has an economic and social base in the technology and the affluence of industrial society that virtually guarantees that millions of young Americans can delay their entrance into culture longer than ever before in history. The "counter-culture" is not, of itself, a revolutionary force. It is simply a large number of young people with a number of years on their hands (perhaps a decade) between adolescence and adulthood. What it is seeking is not a revolution but an institutional umbrella, a sanctuary, a home.

The "movement," meanwhile, arises from the effectiveness of the teaching of Jewish, Christian, humanistic—in a word, personalistic—morality to our young people. Many detest the war in Vietnam and, more than that, the bureaucratic, military, imperial, racist attitudes from which it, in part, springs. With a social and economic base that allows them the luxury of doing what they think they ought to do, a goodly proportion of those in the youth culture—not all, perhaps not even a majority—constitute a significant but frequently unfocused political force

[1] See Peter Berger and Richard Neuhaus, *Movement and Revolution* (New York, 1970).

intent on, for the most part, humane purposes. The movement lacks national leadership; it has neither the discipline, nor the program, nor the endurance of a political party. Its capital of humane morality may easily be squandered.

The radical political groups are a very small minority, even of the movement. They have in a half-dozen short years rendered five or six correct judgments about the course of American and world politics. On the other hand, the radical groups commonly share typical American middle-class deficiencies: impatience, a preference for sentiment and action over intelligence and endurance, a love for the confrontations of *High Noon,* a taste for violence, self-pity, a weakness for taking short-cuts and evading difficulties, anti-intellectualism, a tendency towards slogans and simple solutions, intense sectarianism, a fascination with personal moral purity, and a strange longing for death ("since I probably won't be alive five years from now . . .").

Moreover, the radical groups are: (a) almost utterly isolated from other social classes in American society, with none of whom they have a solid, reliable bond, and (b) too internally disorganized and ideologically confused to make their strong passions effective. It is not by accident that, with so much to be done in this nation, they often find themselves feeling helpless, frustrated, and impotent. Not only do they psychologically crave instant success (unused to failure as they are) and tire easily, but they are also saddled by contradictory, hobbling, and self-defeating bits and pieces of unassimilated (and unassimilable) ideology.

The main strength of the movement, consequently, and *a fortiori* of the more intense radical groups, comes not from any insights, programs, or possibilities of their own. It comes from the grave weaknesses of American society. "Being radicalized" seldom consists in acquiring a new political vision, let alone a program or a strategy. It consists, rather, in coming to see with an intense degree of clarity the weaknesses of "the system." Insofar as it is a "yes," radical politics is an amalgam of traditional (although often minority) American values and (usually quite low-grade) Marxist methods of analysis. But radical politics is not very much of a "yes"; much more centrally, it is a "no" to the system. "Resistance," "dissent," "protest," "No!" are its heavy words.

Thus, during most of 1969, not only the movement but also the smaller radical groups were more or less in total disarray. Leadership, direction, spirit were lacking. Internal sectarian quarrels, frustration, dropping out, and despair characterized the vast majority of those involved.

When President Nixon invaded Cambodia, and above all when four young whites were killed at Kent State, millions felt a new surge of energy, purpose, and unity. The movement is parasitic on its carrier. It has come to depend on its carrier for its own political direction. The movement is not so much a "mover" as a protester of flagrant abuse. It has few plans. It waits, and reacts. The leaders within the movement are not so much activists (strategists, tacticians, trainers, organizers, long-range planners) as sensitive barometers of emotion and articulators of feelings.

Moreover, the riot of the construction workers in New York City was a vivid sign of the intense contempt the middle-class student has driven deep into the heart of lower-middle-class whites. It is a mistake to talk about "right" and "left" in such matters. The workers are just as capable of working in some left-wing directions as students; and some students are just as capable of belligerence, violence, and attacks on free speech as the workers.

What is at stake is the hatred of the uneducated who work with their hands for the sons of the privileged—and who cover their embarrassment at their lack of "culture" with pride in their patriotism, their public decency, and their observance of the social mores. Ashamed of the American flag, dissenting students shame the men whose pride derives from it. Flaunting new indecencies and flagrantly violating established mores, well-off students undercut the sole sources of public pride left to these men.

Disobeying, the privileged seem to accuse of immorality men who proudly identify morality with obedience. Shouting "Pigs!" (it is clear that the cops and workers recognize one another as brothers and friends), the privileged rub raw the deep wound of men who feel uncultivated and less than humane.

The *serious* polarization in American life is not between the generations but between classes. Lower-middle-class students, who need education in order to break out of the class in which they were born, are often fiercely opposed to the more affluent radicals. Disguised under temporary alliances based on mutual weakness, black students and white middle-class radicals are storing up towards each other an immense, deep rage and violent antipathy. (Why all the shock over the deaths of four *white* students? Why the sudden concern about *Cambodia?* Poor blacks can't afford to close the schools.)

The signs of serious, long-range revolutionary intent among radical groups are almost nil, and such signs as do exist are certainly not impressive for their thoughtfulness, their thoroughness, or their nuanced sense of reality. Moreover, the larger movement is so infected with quite classical American prejudices that the "revolution in consciousness" it is supposed to have brought, or to promise, seems clearly to have peaked and to be in decline.

The appearance of a youth culture, however, is a fact with which we shall have to live for a long time. But just because it is a youth culture, it will be both volatile, oscillating, unreliable, and premoral. It is characteristic of youth to be trying various identities on for size, to be experimenting, to enunciate moral ideals in all their purity, and to be imperceptive of the ambiguities of the concrete texture of human life and action. Young people may be exemplars of idealism; they are classically expected to make good troops for causes. They should not be expected to be exemplars of fully moral action, that is, of wisdom-in-action.

The more serious young people today face two severe dangers from their older admirers. First, the romanticism implicit in the liberal tradition has always supposed that the closer to youth, childhood, and the state of the noble savage a person is, the more moral he is. Hence, older people, who should keep their critical poise, are often dazzled by sheer youth, and hardly dare to speak even in the teeth of oracles of nonsense. Secondly, older people who have borne defeats through their own compromises, or even perhaps through their own earlier heroism, sometimes vicariously try again through young people to recapture long-ago feelings of knighthood.

The lessons of the last four decades—the Depression, Hitler, the atom bomb, the cold war—have been particularly chastening to idealists. At some cost, men purposefully instructed themselves in ideological modesty, pragmatism, and limited hopes. (To their efforts, we probably owe our lives.) Many no doubt hanker to be "pure" again and to shuck off the difficult lessons of realism. "Siding with the young" has become cheap grace.

For the vast majority of our generation, the notion of the intellectual life as an end in itself was never more than a "hoary piety." For, in our generation, "relevance" took the form of pragmatism and realism. There were not many who wished to spend their lives in inquiry for its own sake. Among those few, who felt as much a minority than as now, this was no "hoary piety" but life itself.

Moreover, the very notion of inquiry as an end in itself was not often explored in our generation; I, at least, recall having to work out most of its implications for myself. It was not socially comfortable in those days to care too much about one's studies; "grinds" were not popular in the McCarthyite days of anti-intellectualism. "Relevant" fields like the sciences and enginering were multiplying everywhere.

I came to three conclusions. First, unless the university has somewhere among its various novelties and institutes for relevance a cadre of men committed to the demands of critical intelligence, little in the university will be of enduring relevance. Nothing is as irrelevant as the preceding generation's relevance.

A university wholly committed to social and political relevance here and now is more easily co-opted by the establishment of its times. For relevance, in the short term, means "what works"; and its parameters of inquiry are of necessity foreshortened. One could even argue that the Achilles' heel of liberalism after World War II was its insistence on relevance, under the banners of scientific objectivity, pragmatism, and hard-headed realism. The radical cry for relevance seems intent on repeating its fathers' central error.

Secondly, the phrase "critical inquiry for its own sake" does not connote social and political irresponsibility, the ivory tower, or, even, irrelevance. On the contrary, I deem it the most central and the highest social good of *any* society that it free a number of its members for precisely such critical inquiry. Nothing is a greater tribute to human freedom than freedom from utilitarian purposes. Unless there are ends in themselves, sought for their own sake, instrumentalism and manipulation are the only available human life style.

And among candidates for ends in themselves that might be cherished as a social and political good, critical inquiry has the advantage of being endless, cumulative, self-critical, and exploratory. It opens horizons. It enlarges the liberty of all. It brings satisfactions of the spirit, without which no number of Evinrudes, Hondas, fucks, barbiturates, or drops of acid even come close to assuaging the human heart.

Thirdly, critical inquiry may take as its focus not theory for its own sake but wisdom-in-action for its own sake. It is true that the classical philosophical tradition, like the modern scientific tradition, takes theory as its focus, explanation as its main assignment, a sort of objective map of what things are or how they work as its goal. But when I argue that a new epistemology is both possible and necessary, I mean to suggest that one may break with both the classical and scientific tradition and still be faithful to inquiry as an end in itself.

Specifically, one may take human action as one's central field of inquiry. What makes human actions human? What makes them wise, humanistic, good? Is it true that men *never* act according to rational, logical principles but *always* according to a sense of reality, story, symbol? In what ways do their culture and their language act in them? In what ways are their science, theories, art, religion present in their actions? One can make action, not theory, the focal point of one's theory.

Moreover, the theoretician who wishes to understand human action does well, it appears, to place himself in the middle of at least some social and political actions. He does so not as an activist solely, for the sake of immediate relevance alone, but as a theoretician as well, in order to feel in himself and in the social body the pressures, pulls, and heat of action. Theories of action inherited from the past probably draw our attention away from crucial elements in the experience of action; we probably experience action incorrectly.

To develop this notion further would require a great deal more space—in fact, a life's work. Those who are serious about revolutionary changes in American society, and particularly in American education, do well not to rely too much upon the youth culture, the movement, or radical political groups in their present forms.

My own relationship to radical politics is difficult to state. One central point, above all, carries me in the radical direction. Secular liberal humanism—the "modern consciousness" to which we are often told we must conform—has long been my main target. It is, for all its power and achievements, a too-narrow, manipulative, alienating, and destructive form of consciousness. I am not a child of the Enlightenment; its rationalism is only one episode in my psychic life, a beautiful and powerful one, but also a narrow, parochial one.

But neither am I a child of the Reformation. I inherit a long, wise, and Catholic suspicion of enthusiasm—not only of the sort Luther opposed but also of the sort he manifested. An extended discussion of Tillich will bring this out.

When I hear the words "the traditional academic culture," I do not think of Harvard, which is relatively new upon the scene and much given to American forms of relevance, to pragmatism and, intermixed with its genuine and profound humanism, to Tillich's "technological realism." I have always wished to be both ancient and medieval in my sensibilities as well as modern (cf. *Naked I Leave*), on the ground that the standpoints of past ages should be appropriated, cherished and, if transformed, still never merely negated. It is implausible that men in the past were less wise, less clever, less full of love and vitality than we; it is probable that for each of our gains we have suffered losses.

But Tillich's "mystical realism" is not an accurate description of the part of medieval thought that most attracted me. It was precisely the image of Aristotle pointing downward to the earth, here and now, as opposed to Plato's finger pointing towards the heavens that always excited me: The sacramental love of *this* concrete form, *here, now.* God is not "out there."

I thrilled to Gerard Manley Hopkins' notions of Inscape and *Haecceitas,* because that was exactly what I had discovered (which few do) in Aristotle and Aquinas. Catholicism, Chesterton once said, is a thick steak, a glass of stout and a long cigar. I have always felt in my Catholic friends an unfeigned love of this earth and of the concrete singular that is quite different from that of Protestants.

Tillich's "historical realism" and "self-transcending realism," by contrast, seem to me to be *almost* at the heart of the matter, but not quite. Tillich's image of "the thunderstorm at night, when the lightning throws a blinding clarity over all things, leaving them in complete darkness the next moment" exposes the inadequacy. For that image, to my mind, is precisely too Germanic, too ecstatic, too extraordinary, too discontinuous and, finally, too enthusiastic to pass as an accurate image for human wisdom about oneself, the world, and God.

My God is a God of ordinary things, of routine, of the grind and jading of everyday life—of a simple cigar, of a grain of sand, of boredom and tedium and hard work as well as of moments of rapture. One way I test politicians, theoreticians, poets, activists, philosophers, and friends is by how alert they are to the mysteries of the ordinary. The German quest for "ecstasy," "revelation," "faith," "transparency" gives me a certain fear of those abstractions in whose name concrete, complex human organisms are so often crushed.

In 1965–66, consequently, when I first encountered the counter-culture in California (the first editor to see *A Theology for Radical Politics* thought my judgment was being warped by California), it was plain that its instincts were right; that its moral sensitivity, formed by liberal realism, was sharp and hard; and that it had the courage to go for a major cultural breakthrough. Before the radical movement, "moral" meant John Foster Dulles; "being" was a word to scorn; "commitment" was for the softheaded; "objective" was an ideal and "subjective" was pejorative; "community" was hardly known; "celebration" and "myth" and "ritual" were from the benighted Catholic Dark Ages before Reason and Protestantism. I am greatly indebted to a movement that has given breathing space to ideas I loved long before the movement appeared and will love long after it disappears.

As a serious revolutionary movement, however, the counterculture is as full of internal contradictions as America's right wing, whose social and economic origins are remarkably similar. The military right wants less federal centralization *and* more militant anti-Communism abroad; the movement wants leaderlessness, non-organization *and* political effectiveness. Both sides wish us to make an act of faith, in order to believe possibilities that are not even dimly plausible. Both are nostalgic about the American past. Both are astonishingly individualistic, evangelical, given to simple moralizing, committed to *laissez faire* ("do your own thing"), careless with civil liberties. Both love confrontation. Both turn easily to violence out of standard, made-in-USA impatience. "Hanoi won't do our will? Burn it down!" (For "Hanoi" supply any institution antagonistic to one's will.)

For two years now we have found, among those who sang "All power to the imagination!" a limited and sterile imagination, gimmicky, superficial, burdensomely repetitive. To disguise the repetitiveness, some few in the movement have turned to bombs. Well, escalation is the law of the ecstatic spirit. The limits of the human body, of the prickly human character, of human ordinariness and routine and recalcitrance, are exactly what *ek-stasis* is trying to stand outside of. The inner secret of the ecstatic spirit, therefore, is always apocalypse, flames, death. Finite human life can never satisfy it, and is not what it loves: "Burn it down!" The current rash of images of young people going to an early but glorious death in the exact symbolic representation of an inner commitment to abstraction, and thus to death.

If America has grown too powerful for its own wisdom; if our society has grown too large and disconnected and ungov-

148

ernable; if our very values themselves are not humane values, but too narrow, distorted, and arranged in destructive priority; if our society is sick and needs not reform but revolution; then there is more reason than ever for being suspicious of the enthusiasts. Not all who claim to speak for the Holy Spirit—or for History, or for "A New History"—are to be trusted. A revolution is a long-range affair. No spontaneous, ecstatic salvation is about to come. There must be a very long march, and one's ability to endure the length of the march, not a single dramatic burst of action, is the test of human courage.

"There is no time!" we are told. "In five years, or ten, we will all be dead." And who promised us that the world would not come to an end? The use of the end of the world as a homiletic arm-twister annoys me no less in fundamentalist politics than in fundamentalist religion. Every day is a good day for the world to end, and I prefer not to panic, but to live the way I wish to live, day by day. When the alarms are passed, there will still be mouths to feed, including sheepish radical mouths.

Let me, in conclusion, give several indications concerning the spiritual poverty of the counter-culture. The first sign is the cry "the pigs." The function of such a cry is dehumanization; and children advantaged enough to be in college have no humane need to scorn the values, mores, and limitations of the men of the lower-middle class. The second sign is the random, inexplicable outbreaks of violence, unfailingly a sign of *ressentiment,* of an impoverished imagination, of weakness, of self-doubt. The third sign is the gap between public and private utterance. Radicals in public quite often now say one thing, strike one pose, and in private strike quite another.

The fourth sign is the sectarianism; the implicit, ritualistic imposing of loyalty oaths; the quest for purity. The fifth is the easily exposed bad conscience; the unadmitted extent to which the counter-culture is economically parasitic, and the flagrant and open hustling for advantages to which the counter-culture is as conspicuously prone as the culture. The sixth is the fervent cry "revolution" coupled with the outraged cry "repression," as if in surprise. Do revolutionaries expect love, affection, and clemency, too? The seventh is the concentration on "easy targets": middle America, the laborers, the lower-middle class, the professionals are too hard to reach, so "radicalize" *high school* students!

I conclude that Gustav Weigel was right: "All human things, given enough time, go badly." The radical movement squandered its advantages in six brief years. Mass communications fanned it, industry made millions on it, and soon the American spirit, unflinchingly perceived by de Tocqueville, will seek some new diversion. Younger high school students will seek some fresh, easy way to distinguish themselves from their older brothers and sisters. They will note that "consciousness-expanding" drugs expanded few consciousnesses; that the politics of rage sated passions but improved the lot of few of the poor, and diminished the right wing and the armies and the police not at all; and that some older brothers and sisters, full of idealistic slogans, entered middle age unprepared, embittered, isolated, and by-passed.

The counter-culture is not our salvation. It is a system as corrupt and limited as the one it presumes to revolutionize. It is, however, not nearly as complex, deep, or modest as the poor system in which we are all, now, troubled pilgrims. To refashion the ship on which we sail we must be far more creative than our forebears of 1776. Mere reform is not sufficient. The task is not ecstatic, neither is it pragmatic.

Adults have no right, therefore, either in politics or in education, to abdicate their own wisdom, their own responsibility, their own skills for the sentimentality of some swift salvation through youth. The young have borne us precious gifts. But political struggles are won by superior organization, by discipline, by long-range plans. And education is reformed, not by wishfulness, but by better logic, better insight, better judgment, better sensitivity, better imagination than what went before.

Many who write favorably of new visions in education confess that they have only the faintest idea what education in the free counter-culture will look like. For three years I have been gaining some fairly clear notions of what counter-culture education will look like. The prospect is pretty awful. That verification will come for others, too, when they see the fruits by which the tree is to be judged. Let us hope, however, that the tree learns soon to send down deeper roots and gains a longer life.

In this respect, two trends are hopeful. Senator Edward Kennedy received a standing ovation when he told a large audience of students: When you grow tired of marching, demonstrations, picketing, and violence, come back to the real sources of change: electoral politics. First, the youth culture learned that electoral politics doesn't work; then they learned that disruption and demonstration don't work, either. So the wheel has turned. Possibly, many will learn that one defeat is not a whole campaign. Politics is not a field in which terms like "victory" and "defeat" are clear-cut, total, pure.

Secondly, the radical wing has been somewhat discredited— by the perceptible unhappiness of its members, its factionalism, its tantrums, its bombers, and the ruthless tendencies of some of its leaders. Changing the Congress seems to many students a limited but more effective step than tying their emotions to instant revolution. The moral authority on campus has swung away from the extremist radicals and towards the center. It is a propitious moment to forge an organization out of the movement, to give it sharp political focus and electoral clout. Many eager spirits are waiting. Leadership could create a tide that might last a decade. We desperately need political leadership.

16. If This Is the Green Wood . . .

IN 1954, a junior in college, I was struck by a sentence of Maritain's predicting that, despite pragmatism, questions of ethics would be foremost in America's intellectual consciousness in the coming generation. That sentence has been important in key decisions of my life. Recently, I went looking to recover that sentence, and failed. I remembered that Maritain's marvelous Terry Lectures at Yale in 1943 had many anticipations of the "greening of America" now discerned at Yale by Charles Reich, professor of law.[1]

There are, for example, in *Education at the Crossroads,* sentences like the following: "A special danger is now to be mentioned, I mean the danger of an education which would aim, not at making man truly human, but making him merely into an organ of a technocratic society" (p. 113). And again:

What are we fighting for, if the only thing human reason can do is to measure and manage better? If we have no means of determining what freedom, justice, spirit, human personality, and human dignity consist of, and why they are worthy of our dying for them, then we are fighting and dying only for words. If we and the youth who will be educated by future democracies hold everything that is not calculable or workable to be only a matter of myth, and believe only in a technocratic world, then we can indeed conquer Nazi Germany militarily and technically, but we ourselves shall have been conquered morally by Nazi Germany.

For the preface to Fascism and Nazism is a thorough disregard of the spiritual dignity of man, and the assumption that merely material or biological standards rule human life and morality. Thereafter, since man cannot do without some loving adoration, the monstrous adoration of the totalitarian Leviathan will have its day. Technology is good, as a means for the human spirit and for human ends. But technocracy, that is to say technology so understood and so worshiped as to exclude any

[1] *The Greening of America, How the Youth Revolution is Trying to Make America Livable,* New York, 1970.

superior wisdom and any other understanding than that of calculable phenomena, leaves in human life nothing but relationships of force, or at best those of pleasure, and necessarily ends up in a philosophy of domination.

A techno*cratic* society is but a totalitarian one. But a techno*logical* society may be democratic, provided this society is quickened by an inspiration which is supra-technological, and if it recognizes, with Bergson, that "the body, now larger, calls for a bigger soul," and that "the mechanical" summons up "the mystical" (pp. 114–115).

Maritain prepared many of us for the radical, anti-liberal turn in American politics in recent years. He pointed us—from within the Thomistic context in which our minds first tested themselves —towards the possibilities and benefits of American naturalism and pragmatism; but he also exposed the too-weak foundations of democratic liberalism. In the years that intervened between 1950 (when I first discovered, with joy, the spirit of Maritain) and 1970, like many others, I departed in many ways from Maritain's horizon. I like to think that there has been an inner fidelity, however, to the intentional thrust he gave us now so long ago.

Such reflections are constantly forced upon me when I try to consider why I find the ending of the liberal era exhilarating, but also find the radical movement woefully superficial. Perhaps many others today experience a similar solitude. Too little, in any case, is written about the real solitude in which so many in our profession labor today—a solitude not assuaged by frequent trips by air and auto to conferences, symposia, and editorial meetings.

Charles Reich's valuable book is of a genre familiar to Catholics. It is a record of a conversion, a set of reflections set in train by Reich's "change of consciousness" in the summer of 1967 in the hot, clear California sun in Berkeley. It is not only a conversion book. It is also a new convert's program for missionary activity—how to carry the new consciousness to "workers and older people" (Chapter X). It is, finally, a pastoral book: full of the warm, optimistic concern of a priestly man for his newly discovered *pusillus grex,* his weak, lamb-like flock so sorely set up upon by the age.

And yet again, it is the record of a conversion *from* a form of consciousness quite clearly limited, described, and set forth—liberal, meritocratic, pragmatic. The heart of Reich's book is a description of three kinds of consciousness in American life, and a mythic construction which he calls the Corporate State. First, there are the three consciousnesses. ("Consciousness," because "reason" is too narrow a word for what is at stake. The shift to "consciousness" from "reason" is what will distinguish the political ethic of our generation from that of, say, Niebuhr and Bennett, Lippmann and Morgenthau.)

Consciousness I is related to pre-industrial America: its individualism, its sense of human corruptibility, and its commitment to "character" and hard work. Consciousness II is related to the new technologies of the planned economy, its sense of human rationality and its commitment to expertise, excellence, a system of merit, and professionalization. Consciousness III is related to the new age of affluence, its sense of human fragility, but also its commitment to "the promise"—the promise of human technology, human goodness, and human possibility.

From the pre-industrial age it can take the integration and balance of life, the sense of God in everything. From the industrial era it can take technology and the steady rise to a higher level of life. From its own age, it can take the control and use of technology, and the way of life of satisfaction, community, and love, a way of life that aspires higher and higher, without forgetting its human source. . . . And it will do so within a society that makes the Judeo-Christian ethic not merely an ignored command, but a realistic way of life (p. 390).

The general scheme suggests the developments Maritain foretold. Yet it is remarkable that none of the three forms of consciousness quite expresses the form of consciousness ordinarily familiar to Catholics. Reich's prose in the description of Consciousness I is wooden, as if he is describing something of which he has no inner experience—only what he has gleaned from newspaper accounts and fleeting encounters. By contrast, strong emotions surge beneath his prose when he describes Consciousness II—particularly in its academic settings, its dryness, its well-planned summers in interesting and cosmopolitan environments. His story is a story of a journey from II to III.

It is a story proper to an American elite. "The new generation, who ardently desire social change, are largely members of America's affluent ruling class" (p. 308). Reich's perception, here, is perhaps led into exaggeration by his viewpoint from Yale. Many members of America's lower classes—Jewish, Catholic, and Protestant—are also prominent in the counter-culture. Not all share Reich's relationship to Consciousness II. Reich seems related to it as "insider" (a "fallen-away liberal"), but many in Consciousness III are related to Consciousness II through the resentment, envy, or merely ignorance of outsiders.

Feelings in Consciousness III run very high. Sympathetically, one can describe the movement as affirmative, for love and community and openness and swift acceptance. But one must also account for furious resentments, suddenly flashing rage, and the unquenchable hatred that also characterize almost everyone in Consciousness III in certain characteristic situations. Consciousness III is known for its gentleness at Woodstock, but also for its furies and obscenities and irrational eruptions.

Reich is careful to point out all the deficiencies of Consciousness I and Consciousness II; and he often draws into their delineation elements that those who live in such forms of consciousness would describe as fallings away from their own ideals. When he describes Consciousness III, he is kind, gentle, and relentlessly concentrated upon its ideal form. The result is that we get one ideal type pitted against two types in which actualities are also included.

Moreover, the three types are fitted into an evolutionary scheme of such a sort that normative force is brought to bear upon the reader: You *ought* to share in Consciousness III. It is more advanced, more humane, more practical, more free, more moral, more pleasant, and so forth. The clear implication of immorality, obsolescence, and irrelevance is laid against persons not sharing Consciousness III. Beware of those who claim to belong to Higher Types! Sectarianism, emphasis on ideological purity, intolerance, and endemic restlessness are suppressed in Reich's description of Consciousness III, but latent in what he describes. He fails to note chronic symptoms of dependency and infantilism that often appear.

Consciousness III, in fact, is already being surpassed. Reich realizes that tentativeness of what he describes and tries to make a virtue of it by calling it a form of "openness" and risk. One might just as accurately call it superficiality. Whoever lives by impulse, instinct, and feeling necessarily "blows as the wind blows, yes and is mobile." Consciousness III describes as "authentic existence" fidelity to one's dominant emotion of the moment. It resists loyalty, long-term commitments, promises, and obligations (p. 228). To an extent, this definition is a form of self-defense temporarily necessary for many, in the most disciplined, hurried, and closely tracked generation in history; but one ought not to forget that it is also the definition of fickleness.

Consciousness III is being surpassed because it encounters realities for which it is not prepared. One can give all for Bobby Seale, but the sordidness of the underworld of Black Pantherdom cannot, finally, be idealized away. And all along the edges (and not only on the edges) of those who share Consciousness III is rapacity; an unsurpassed talent for the hustling and con-artistry so typical of America's underbelly; madness; depression; an incapacity for sustained human relations; fits of rage; murder; and even cannibalism. "There are no 'tough guys' among the youth of Consciousness III." Reich limits himself in describing Consciousness III to its most faithful, in their most demonstrative acts of generosity. He even excludes the more politically oriented; he excludes motorcycle boys, beach rats, and groups like the Manson gang. His is an elitist description, biased not only by class but by taste and orientation.

Consciousness III derives its primal emotions, Reich well notes, from an indescribable anger. "A key word in understanding its origin is *betrayal*." To the young "the discrepancy between what could be and what is, is overwhelming; perhaps it is the greatest single fact of their existence. . . . They feel the betrayal in excruciatingly personal terms" (p. 220). One *could* say that they were brought up by parents who valued them as persons, treated them more reasonably, prized their individuality, and protected them from disease, chaos, and pain more thoroughly than any generation in history—by parents, also, who were children of the Enlightenment, and believed in Reason, Progress, and human goodness. As Kurt Vonnegut puts it in *Mother Night*, the toys they played with did not teach them nearly enough about the aggressiveness, skepticism, and hostility necessary for survival on earth.

". . . The young radicals show a *continuity* of ideals from childhood on; they simply stayed with them while their parents failed to" (p. 221). In a word, the children repeat the illusions of the parents. No more than their parents have they attained a tragic view of life. They remain optimistic, innocent, Adamic Americans to the end. And thus they prepare yet another cycle of American irrationality and violence. For the truly overwhelming innocence and optimism of Americans, which Reich shares to a breathtaking degree, cannot easily sustain the inevitable defeats and stringently limited victories which life, in fact, allows. It is no assertion of Consciousness I merely, or of Consciousness II, that life is tragic: it is the overwhelming conviction of the entire human race, learned in immense travail, bloodshed, and irrationality through every generation, including our own.

Lacking a sense of tragedy, Americans of whatever consciousness expect too much from life. "Given an abundance of material goods," Reich writes, believing like Richard Nixon in the goodness of the American heart, "the possibilities of a human community are finally made real, for it is now possible to believe in the goodness of man" (p. 354). We are all of us, in our most American moments, Gatsbys, Thomas Wolfes, Walt Whitmans pursuing far-off lights, tunnels, secret doors. We believe, in our unguarded moments, in an earthly paradise. And with each devastating human lesson—the massacre of the Indians, the incomparably bloody Civil War, the sustained brutalization of black consciousness, Prohibition and organized crime, pollution, Vietnam, the terror-bombing of America—we turn aside from the obvious conclusion. "Up ahead," we say, "if only we begin again, become once more as little children." Pursuing paradise, Americans in every generation have intensified the fires of their own peculiar hell.

The breaking of the cycle will not come through yet one more springtime of old illusions which, as surely as the others, aims at violence. The breaking of the cycle is a recognition of brokenness, of only partial victory, of the inevitability of betrayal, of the untrustworthiness of everything human. These are not

Calvinistic or even Christian admonitions. They are the deepest convictions of Buddhists, Hindus, Moslems, Aztecs—in a word, of the entire human race. "Life," Buddha says, "is suffering." Americans are mad. The greening of that little light of illusion up ahead is not a hopeful sign; it is a sign of blood.

Consciousness III expects far too much of life, of institutions, of their parents, of themselves. The illusion of human perfectibility only prepares an ultimate sense of guilt. Thus Reich invents a myth duly capitalized as "The Corporate State" which serves as a projection of all that ails us. *We* are good. Only the power of the State prevents us, due to cultural lag, from being what we could be. Much that he has to say about the Corporate State is descriptive of something new, as Galbraith argued in *The New Industrial State*. But much of it could also be said of human arrangements at any time in human history. Reich consistently writes as if there were, some time earlier, before now, a *better* time. His essential vision is that "the human condition, if that is what it is, has been getting steadily worse in the Corporate State" (p. 220). His image is *downhill*, just as the images of Consciousness I and II were "Everything is looking *up*."

The two images cry out to each other as abyss to abyss. Life is indeed a pilgrimage. But "better" or "worse"? How shall these be measured? Perhaps for certain elites, life in America in 1970 is worse than in 1870. Many other families can only marvel at the opportunities, the liberty, and the possibility they have by comparison with what their grandfathers had. And, on the other hand, who is to say that the ordinary Angeleno of 1970 is a better man than his predecessor of 1870 in California's hardy days?

The evidence Reich submits for the heretofore unperceived encroachments of a Corporate State—in which economics, politics, and culture itself are so closely interlocked at to be more unified than ever—is so loose as to be capable of many mythical interpretations. There are some hoary Catholic sages who have long argued that life has been going downhill since the thirteenth century. (Reich, in fact, offers unprecedented consolation to those accustomed to hearing from American scholars only a pejorative use of "medieval.")

One might argue that the myth of "Progress" is untenable. For every advance a price is paid. For technology, we pay the price of the rationalization of life. For science, we pay the price of a world of prediction and control. For enlightenment, we pay the price of alienation from our emotions, from our bodies, and from one another. For protection from disease, the ravages of nature, and poverty, we pay the price of vulnerability to our own irrationality. Men in the Middle Ages feared famine, storm, and plague; we fear riot, warfare, pollution, self-destruction. Those who believe in an earthly paradise heap guilt upon men for not attaining it; for secularization, too, we have paid a price in the source of guilt.

Reich gives many fresh insights into the American cultural situation, which only a lawyer could have contributed: that the new form of property is not land nor ownership, but status and privilege and license; that law has replaced money as the medium which enables act and power and functioning. But just where he might follow these insights with specific diagnosis and specific invention of new social controls, he falls silent. He adopts the mood of evasion. He points to Vietnam, the election of 1968, and the unchallenged development of chemical Mace as critical examples ending all possibility of ordinary political discussion. His appeal to "change consciousness first" sounds far too like Billy Graham—only more dangerously so. If our brilliant elites neglect changing laws in order to concentrate on "changing hearts and minds," whence will political creativity come?

Politics is not merely a matter of helping a "system" to keep moving. Politics is also a vocation to invent new systems, and constantly to be reshaping as large and basic a part of systems as human ingenuity can reach. Power does come from the barrel of symbols (as *The Experience of Nothingness* puts it). But Reich goes too far when he asserts that "consciousness is prior to structure" (p. 334). In some ways it is: inventive and restless spirits set in motion new inventions and currents of expectation which ultimately become institutionalized. In other ways it isn't: structures in their emerging and in their breaking down stimulate persons to restlessness, inquiry, striving. Thus, for example, the technology generated by the Second World War altered the environment in which Consciousness II found, at first, its verification and eventually its limitations; and in which Consciousness III, without yet knowing whither or why, has become extraordinarily ill at ease.

We are called upon to invent new procedures, new methods, new professions, new directions for affectivity and striving and inquiry. The task is not merely one of placing "a supreme value on the development of consciousness, sensitivity, experience, knowledge" (p. 336). Decadent elites have frequently done that. The task is also one of inventing political forms, not always *de novo*, like some Venus appearing from the sea, but with whatever material, in whatever way, we have at hand. The politically wise love the real, the concrete, the here and now, not for its own sake but as the touchstone against illusion.

The war in Vietnam, the election of 1968, and the unsupervised and unexamined use of Mace do not in fact prove what the easily discouraged too easily conclude from them. It is not only "the system" that failed. It failed in precise ways, at precise places. And *we the people* failed, collectively, and in all our associated sub-groups. Those who could have avoided or ended the war in Vietnam most directly (Johnson, Rusk, Rostow, *et al.*) were emotionally and by moral conviction committed to the prosecution of the war. The peace movement, which made startling and rapid political progress, committed egregious mistakes in alienating potential political allies. The failure was political, not mystical or moral.

Similarly with the election of 1968. Robert Kennedy understood the political problem of convincing the delegates and not merely the electorate. It is not, I think, a poor political system, but a sound one, which interposes representatives between the people and their popular sentiment at any time. To his credit, Lyndon Johnson did not pull out all the stops of jingoism available to him to create war fever in the electorate; some, yes, but not all. And Eugene McCarthy and others did not do a good enough job in getting to the delegates more persuasively than Humphrey. We, of our generation, having a potential popular majority, lacked the competence to forge a political instrument of our will. To blame our stars rather than ourselves is understandable, but not admirable.

160

The election of 1968 showed only that emotions and amateur-ishness exceeded our capacity for strategy, concentration, and coolness. We failed. Will we do the same in 1972? And 1976? And then blame it again on "the system"? With a very poor and uncharismatic personality, and with only a minority of popular support, Richard Nixon defeated us by sheer competence. We have to be better than he is, and so far we aren't. Better not only at gaining power (although that's what makes a "system" move in a direction) but also at diagnosis and concrete political creation. We must *invent* a new system step by step.

One key to our failure lies in the huge perceptual gap that separates us from the American people and especially from the worker. Our fantasies—seldom plainer than in that abominable and meretricious film *Joe*—are vile. Thus Reich himself, urging us to be more *generous* in our attitudes towards the plumbers, gas station attendants, and truck drivers around us:

Look again at a "fascist"—tight-lipped, tense, crew cut, correctly dressed, church-going, an American flag on his car window, a hostile eye for communists, youth, and blacks. He has had very little of love, or poetry, or music, or nature, or joy. He has been dominated by fear. He has been condemned to narrow-minded prejudice, to a self-defeating materialism, to a lonely suspicion of his fellow men. He is angry, envious, bitter, self-hating. He ravages his own environment. He has fled all his life from consciousness and responsibility. He is turned against his own nature; in his agony he has recoiled upon himself. He is what the ma-chine left after it had its way.

The margins of my book carry an anguished *EEE!* at the igno-rance displayed by this passage—and not a few others.

In a word, Consciousness III is not salvation. It is not heaven on earth. It is another place in the pilgrimage of some, a stage along the way: innocent and dangerous, full of the blooming seeds of its own corruptions. Reich's book will help many an elite parent understand the speech of many an elite child. Such "communication" as will then ensue is better than estrangement. But it is not yet a sign of a new spring in America. If it is like this in the green wood, and worse in the dry, we must yet push on elsewhere in search of wisdom and political effectiveness.

In an interview in *The New York Times,* Reich is quoted as saying that his next book will deal with how to change political structures. Now *that* will be the text! We can't, as Reich says, "just sit in the trees and play harmonicas." . . . Reminds one of the move from liturgy to social action, doesn't it?